A *Forgiving* HEART

STEPHANI L. HASKINS

authorHOUSE®

AuthorHouse™
1663 Liberty Drive
Bloomington, IN 47403
www.authorhouse.com
Phone: 1 (800) 839-8640

Published by AuthorHouse   07/06/2015

ISBN: 978-1-5049-2172-5 (sc)
ISBN: 978-1-5049-2171-8 (e)

Print information available on the last page.

CONTENTS

Chapter 1

THE CALL

Shrugging out of her coat, she hung it in the coat closet. Walking into the dimly lit living room, she sat on a chair. Folding her hands and bowing her head, she began to pray. "Lord, give me the strength I need. Let me love my children and my husband the way fit for you. Lift up..." Before she could finish she heard a thud. Walking to the bottom of the staircase that led to the bedrooms where he children and husband were sleeping. Starting to quickly walk up the stairs, she heard the thud again. Slowing her pace as her heart began to pound hard against her ribs and her chest feeling like it would burst at any moment, she began praying.

"Lord, give me the strength to face whatever it may be. Lord, give me the courage to stand tall and have no fear. Send your angels to guide every move. Protect us dear Lord." She was at the top of the staircase now, standing in the hall. Without turning on any lights, she slowly started walking to the children's rooms. "I am going to check and make sure that the children have not fallen out of bed..." She told herself. "And then I will check on Carl." As she slowly opened the door to Hailley's room, she walked in an took a look around.

Not seeing anything, she pulled the covers a little more snug around Hailley, kissed her on the forehead and went to the door. Turning the doorknob, she looked back to a beautiful, curly, blond hair, blue eyed little girl. Slowly shutting the door, releasing the doorknob as to be as quiet as she possibly could. Leaning against the hallway wall, she said a silent quick prayer. "Thank you Lord for watching over dear Hailley, and thank you for being with her." Not a moment to soon she heard the thud again. Pushing herself from the wall, and turning to the left towards her son's room.

Kerry only had to take but ten steps and she was at the door. Slowly she turned the handle and pushed the door open soundlessly. She looked in and saw Jacob sitting up on his bed. She said his name, "Jacob." No answer. She tried again. "Jacob, honey, it's mommy." Still no answer. Kerry walked over to the side of his bed and then tried again. "Jacob, it's mommy. Did you have a bad dream?" Jacob looked over at Kerry and started crying. "Mommy, it was horrible." Kerry could sense that something wasn't quite right. "Tell me all about it honey. Everything is going to be ok." Jacob turned on his bed and looked her straight in the eyes as he said, "He was big mommy. He had dark eyes and dark hair. He was bigger than daddy, and had hair on his face like daddy. Mommy, I was running as fast as I could and he was chasing me. When he was about to grab me, I woke up."

Jacob was more calm now because he told Kerry everything. "Jacob. Did daddy let you watch a scary movie?" "Daddy said it would be ok but he did tell me that I would get scared." "Jacob. The people in the movies just act. Meaning it is pretend. It isn't real darling. Do you think that you would feel better if I prayed with you?" "Please pray with me." Kerry looked at Jacob with love and compassion in her eyes as she said, "Jacob, do you know that God knows what we want and need before we even ask?" "Yes mommy, I do. I would still feel better if we prayed about it though." Kerry pulled him close in her arms and held his hand. "Mommy, will you also that God tells that man to leave me alone and to leave my dreams?" Kerry was aw struck.

As Kerry was praying, Jacob would squeeze her hand every time he heard his mom praying about taking the man away. Kerry noticed this and felt really good, that little Jacob, only being four years old, had so much faith already. This really touched Kerry's heart. When Kerry was done praying, she gave Jacob's hand a little squeeze of her own. She brushed back the hair that hung loosely around his face and kissed him on the forehead before releasing what she called, "his wild main." Kerry gave Jacob a big hug and told him that it was time to lay down and try to rest now. "Jacob, I think that you will be able to rest better now. Don't you?" "Oh yes mommy." Kerry stood up and laid Jacob back down, tucked him comfortably back in, and gently kissed him one more time on the forehead and then his cheek. They said goodnight and as Kerry reached the door to Jacob's room, she turned back and asked, "Jacob, by any chance did you hear a couple thuds before I came in?"

Jacob gave a little giggle, and then stopped realizing that his mother was being serious. "Yes mom." "Jacob, honey, do you know what it was?" Kerry asked in a concerned yet loving way. "I'm sorry. I kept falling back and hitting my head on that..." Jacob was pointing to the headboard. Kerry let out a sigh of relief. "Mommy, where's daddy?" Kerry looked back at Jacob and said, "Ok honey, thank you and your father is asleep. Something that you should be doing also." "Ok mommy. Goodnight and I love you." "I love you to Jacob darling."

Kerry saw that Jacob was going to fall asleep, so she turned the doorknob, and slowly and quietly shut the door, as she did with Hailley's. Kerry took in a deep breath and released it. Slowly she slid down the wall to a kneeling position. As she did she was praying. The hallway was carpeted, so she didn't hear her husband approaching. When he reached her, he slowly and softly touched her right shoulder. As he did she jumped back against the wall and to the left, away from him. As Kerry looked up she saw that it was just Carl. "Carl, you scared me. I...I was just..." "I know." Carl said as he knelt down to be eye level with Kerry. His eyes looking at hers, as if trying to comfort her in some way. "I didn't mean to interrupt, but I heard people talking. I came to check on the children and saw you out here with your head down. Are you ok love?" He asked. "Yes. I am fine, but Jacob had a bad dream..." Carl looked at her as if he knew what she was going to say next. "So I went in and prayed with him. You know Carl..." "Uh oh, here it comes." He thought to himself. "you really shouldn't let him watch scary movies. You know how he gets." "Yes Kerry, I do. I didn't think it would be bad because there was no blood, no violence, no swearing, nothing. I guess that we stick to cartoons for Jacob then huh?" "I guess so." Carl was looking at Kerry with a look of regret. "I'm sorry dear." "It's ok. Let's go to bed because I am really tired and had a long day at work. I just want to relax." "Ok honey." Carl said as he helped Kerry to her feet.

As Kerry and Carl was getting ready for bed, Kerry gasped. "What is it Kerry?" Carl asked and was at her side in no time. "I'm feeling a little sick because i Have forgotten to turn the security system on." Kerry said with a worried look on her face. "No worries. I will go take care of the issue right now." So Carl rushed out. Kerry finished getting ready for bed as Carl was turning on the security system. She brushed her straight, white teeth, and her long, brown hair. Kerry climbed into bed and was waiting for Carl. Five minutes later, Carl comes back into the room. "Carl, what took you so long?" "Well, for starters, I turned on the security system, made sure the front and back doors were locked, and pad locked the garage door. Carl said with a look of contempt. "Oh yeah, I almost forgot. I also made sure that the children's windows were locked." Carl smirked. "I thought that I might have lost you or something." Kerry said with a gallant twinkle in her eyes and a little smile on her face.

"You know how I am. Always looking after the family. That is my duty as a husband, a father and that is also what I do for a living." Carl smiled and climbed into bed after brushing his teeth. "I know dear. You are always good at what you do. Thank you very much for looking out for us." Kerry said as she drew closer to Carl. "I love you." Carl said with the longing of love and compassion in his eyes for her. "I love you to Carl." Kerry said, looking up into his big, beautiful, baby blue eyes. Kerry pushed a piece of brown hair that was almost in his eyes and gave him a kiss. Taking either side of Kerry's face in both his hands, he brought her face to his, meeting halfway he touched his lips to hers.

"Goodnight my dear sweet Kerry." "Goodnight my love." Kerry said. A few hours after falling asleep (one o'clock a.m.) Carl's pager went off. Drowsily, Carl rolled over, turned on the bedside lamp and checked it.

It was his boss. "Kerry it's my boss. I have to call him back." "Go ahead honey. That is part of your job." Kerry said dreading the fact that it was his boss. Kerry and Carl both knew that his boss only called if there was an emergency or if something serious was going on. Carl picked up the phone that was on the night stand and dialed the number. "Sheriff Fang, it's Carl Benton. You paged?...Really, where?...Give me an hour and I will be there... Thanks Sheriff. Bye." Carl closed his eyes and said a quick little prayer. "Carl honey, do you really have to go?" Kerry didn't want to ask but she really wanted to know. "Yes dear. I do. You know that is part of the job of being sheriff. You have to go. You and I don't want me to go, even I know that, but I have to." Carl looked behind him at Kerry who was looking at him with pleading eyes not to go. "I have to get ready now."

Kerry reached out and grabbed his arm before he got up and asked, "Carl Benton..." She usually only used his first and last name when she was mad at him. "Promise me that you will make it home safe." Kerry's eyes began to water. "Oh honey. Please don't cry. Now you know that question isn't fair because you and I both know that I am not able to make that promise to you. I wish that I could love but I am unable to. I'm sorry." Carl replied with a hint of regret in his voice. "Yes dear. I know." Was all Kerry could find herself to say. Carl took a shower, got into uniform and went back over to Kerry, kissed her goodbye and then he told her that he loved her. "Carl. I love you. I really hope that you know that I pray for you all the time to be safe." "Yes dear. I know. I love you to. Prayers always help with a job like mine. Thank you Kerry." "Be safe Carl." "I don't think that you really need to tell me to be safe. I think that it is the other people that you need to tell to watch out for me." Carl said with a smile. With that all being said he kissed her again and then headed out.

Kerry lay in bed awake for another hour, praying for her husbands protection. At three o'clock a.m. Kerry finally fell asleep. It seemed as if Kerry just blinked and it was already time to get up. Eight o'clock a.m., Jacob comes in, jumping on the bed and waking Kerry up from a dead sleep. "Good morning my little jumping bean. How did you sleep last night?" Kerry looked at him with the loving eyes of a mother who didn't get enough sleep. "I slept good. Where's daddy?" Jacob stopped jumping and was now sitting down waiting for an answer. Kerry sat up on her left elbow, and her head perched on the palm of her hand and said, "Daddy got called into work late last night. Where is your sister?" "She is downstairs watching cartoons." Jacob replied. Kerry smiled at him and then gently placed her hand on his shoulder and said, "Why don't you go down and join her. I will be down to fix breakfast as soon as I get dressed."

"Ok mommy." Jacob stated as he was climbing off the bed. He closed the door behind him when he left the room. While Kerry was getting ready for the day she heard the phone ring. Hailley got to it before she did. Hailley called from the bedroom door, "Mom, the phone is for you." "Thank you Hailley. I will get it in here." Kerry went over and picked up the cordless phone that was on the night stand and answered it. "Hello...are you sure?... When?... How?... We will be there as soon as we can. Thanks for calling." Kerry hung up the phone and set it back down on the night stand. Tears started rolling freely down her cheeks. She knelt beside the bed begging God to have compassion. She prayed for about ten minutes before getting up and finishing getting ready for the day. Tears still stinging her eyes as she worked. Taking a few deep breaths and looking into the mirror at her red eyes, she walked over to the door to the bedroom.

Slowly going down the staircase, holding onto the railing, trying to calm herself down. Walking past the children in the family room watching cartoons, Kerry said, "Good morning Hailley. Jacob, please back up from the television." Jacob groaned as he moved to the couch. "Good morning mom." Kerry was making breakfast for the kids. When she was almost done, she asked Hailley to come set the table. "Hailley. Will you please come set the table for yourself, Jacob and I?" Hailley groaned as usual. "Yes mom." During breakfast, Kerry told the kids to get ready for the day because she was going to take them out. The kids finished eating their bacon, scrambled eggs and pancakes and went upstairs to get ready. Kerry walked over to the stairs and hollered up to the kids, "Dress comfortably because we are going to be out all day."

Kerry walked back to the kitchen to finish putting the dishes into the dishwasher. After she was finished with that she started wiping the table off. Jacob comes running in. "I'm ready." Jacob had on a baseball cap with the L.A. Lakers logo on it, a red sweater with dark blue jeans. "Ok honey. Now go get your shoes on please." "Yes mom." Jacob said while turning around to head for the coat closet. When Hailley came down, she was wearing a pair of plad pajama pants and a loose fitting, white and purple sweater on. "You could have at least put pants on Hailley." Kerry said looking at her. "You told us to dress comfortable. So I did." Kerry looked down and saw that Hailley at least took the time to put on shoes. "Alright. Everyone in the car." Kerry said as she went to the closet to grab a pair of shoes for herself, and then Kerry walked out the door and locked it behind her.

The kids were getting into the car when Kerry walked up. "I'll help Jacob dear. Go ahead and get in. Thank you Hailley." Hailley was big enough to sit without a car seat. Jacob could get into his booster by himself but still had to have help getting buckled. After

Kerry finished buckling Jacob in, she closed the door. "Good morning Mrs. Benton and how are you?" Mr. Kline said from across the other side of the gate. "Mr. Kline has got to be the noisiest neighbor we have around for at least six blocks." Kerry thought before answering him. "I could be doing a lot better, but thanks for asking though." Kerry said in a tone that would be a dead give away that she really didn't want to talk. "How are those children of yours?" Mr. Kline asked moving a little closer to the gate. "Look Mr. Kline. I don't want or even mean to sound rude, but I am in a hurry. Something happened last night and I really have to go." Kerry said, hoping that did the trick and that he would finally give up. "Have a good day." Kerry said while walking over and getting into the car.

Starting the engine to get the car a little warmer. She started to put on her seatbelt when she realized that Mr. Kline was starring at her, watching her. Kerry was feeling a little uneasy about this, so she hurried to finish putting the car in reverse she started backing out of the driveway. Before pulling onto the road, she turned on the radio to Spirit 105.3F. Mm and then started on their way. Before reaching the freeway, Jacob asked from the back seat, "Mommy, where are we going?" Hailley then added in a swift haste, "Yeah mom. I heard you tell Mr. Kline that something happened last night and we had to hurry." Kerry swallowed a knot that was in her throat before answering. "Hailley, Jacob. I wish that I could say that I fibbed to Mr. Kline to get out of talking to him. Which would have been wrong but still. I also wish that I could say that I was taking you to the park or the zoo or something, but I am not able to. The place we are going is…" Kerry paused for a moment. Jacob asked in a sincere way, "Mommy. Why are you crying? Please stop crying." Kerry took a deep breath trying to calm down and stop the tears that were flowing freely now, stinging her eyes making it very difficult to see. "We are headed to the hospital. Your daddy was shot several times last night in a big shoot out down at Central Station."

Kerry turned off the radio now to hear what the children had to say about it. Hailley gasped. Placing her left hand over her mouth for a moment and then taking Jacob's left hand in her right, she began to pray for healing. Hailley finished praying as they were pulling into a spot at the hospital. Kerry put the car in park and then cut the engine, took her seatbelt off and turned around in her seat to face the kids. "I don't know if we will be able to see daddy right away but we have to be strong and that means trying to keep from crying. I know that it is and will be hard but we have to try ok? Please kids?" Both Hailley and Jacob nodded in agreement. "How ever long it takes for daddy to get better, we will wait." Kerry said and again both children nodded. Jacob asked through sobering sobs, "How long will daddy be here mommy?" Kerry looked at him and then reached back and gently laid a hand on his knee and said, "Jacob honey. I am not sure, but how ever long, we will wait. Right baby?" "Yes mommy." Kerry took Jacob's hand in one hand and Hailley's in the other as they walked to the emergency room doors. They reached the clerks desk, Kerry softly asked the lady, "What room is Sheriff Benton in?" "If you will take a seat I will page a doctor to come and speak with you." "Thank you mam."

Kerry, Hailley and Jacob walked over to the waiting room and on the far wall they saw five empty seats, so they took three of them. Sitting there waiting in eager anticipation seemed like forever, but it was really only ten minutes. Kerry saw a young man in a doctor coat walk out, chat with the lady at the desk and then start walking towards them. "Mrs. Benton?" The doctor asked as he approached. He had somewhat of a southern accent. "Yes. This is me." "May I talk with you a moment?" "Yes, my husband, how is he?" Kerry asked eagerly. "My name is doctor Curtis. I examined your husband upon arrival. He suffered from four gun shots." Kerry gasped, putting an arm around both Jacob and Hailley. "Don't worry. I believe he will recover quite well. The first shot was to the leg. Right hip to be exact. If all goes well, he will walk just fine. If not then he will have a slight limp. The second shot was to the left shoulder. Chipped a bone, but, her will recover nicely.

The third shot skimmed his face (right side). We will be doing a tiny skin graph to cover that up though. The fourth shot was an abdominal shot. Lucky for him it didn't hit any vital organs." Kerry was looking at the doctor with tears now streaming down her face. Getting that kind of news was like getting hit by a Mac truck and then someone saying that it will all be ok. The doctor continued. "He should recover quite well and have no serious side effects. He will be as good as new and ready to return to work in about ten weeks tops." "When are we able to see him Dr. Curtis?" Kerry asked in eagerness. "I'm sorry mam, but at this point he needs to rest. He has had a lot done to him and a lot of medication that is making him drowsy." Kerry looked at him as if she was talking to a brick wall. "You didn't answer my question sir. I asked when we were able to see him?"

"Mam. I know that this is a lot to take in for you..." Then he looked at the kids and pointed to both of them, "and the children, but he really needs to rest. If you give us a good six to eight hours he should be up. You might be able to see him then." "I will be back in six hours and I would like to see him. If he is not up, then we will sit there and wait for him to wake." Kerry said in a stern voice, letting the doctor know that she was serious. "Ok mam. I will let the desk clerk and all the nurses know. I know that this is a tragedy. I'm gratefully sorry. If Carlos wakes up sooner, then I will have a nurse give you a call. I don't foresee that happening, but then again you never know. He seems like a very strong man. If you go to the police station, I'm sure that they can and will give you all the information."

Everyone stood up. Kerry shook hands with the doctor and said, "Thank you so much for everything. I'm sorry for my short temper..." The doctor cut her off. "No need for apologies mam. I truly understand." The doctor turned and started walking away, as did

Kerry, Hailley and Jacob. When they were outside Kerry asked, "Do you guys want to spend some time with Aunt Kim and Uncle Bill?" Jacob was the first to answer. "I do. I do." Kerry smiled and then Hailley asked, "Is this a trick question mom? I want to stay with you." Hailley had a disgusted look on her face. "Hailley. I really need some time to think. I also need to get some things straightened out. Besides, I would like to do some digging of my own on what happened." "Oh, all right." Hailley starred out the window the whole car ride and Jacob sang his ABC's. Kerry was just thinking on who it could have been to do something like this.

When they arrived at Kim and Bill's house, Jacob ran inside like he owned the place. Hailley still sat in the car wondering if she really wanted to stay or not. Kerry was telling Kim and Bill all about what happened. "Carl was shot four times and is now in the hospital. I am headed to the police station right now to get details and some more information. I will be back when I am on the way back to the hospital to pick the kids up ok?" Kerry said, eyes filling with tears again as she was talking. Kim gave her a hug to try and comfort her. "Oh sweetie. I am so sorry to hear that. Do you want me to go with you?' Kim asked. Kerry simply said, "No, but thank you. I really need time to think and to get things straightened out and I think best when I'm alone in a quiet place."

Hailley opened the car door and grudgingly walked into the house. She knew it was what her mom wanted was to be alone. "If you need anything, and I mean anything, please call." Bill spoke with a stern yet sympathetic tone in his voice. He reached over and brought his sister Kerry to him and gave her a comforting as it could get hug that Kerry needed. "I will do that. Thank you very much." Kerry took a step back from Bill, took a couple deep breaths and then said goodbye. Kerry then got into her car and took off. Kerry was doing pretty good on not crying until she was near the police station. The nearer she got the more the tears came. Almost as if on queue or something. Kerry pulled into the parking lot and sat there after parking for a good amount of time. She really wanted to know exactly what happened but she couldn't stop crying for her to be able to even see clear enough to walk to the doors.

Kerry started praying that answers would be revealed and that they would find the person responsible for shooting her husband. After a good while longer she regained strength, courage and stopped crying. She told herself she had to be strong, not only for herself but for Carl and the children. Kerry had to pull herself together. Kerry got out of the car, locked it and started walking to the doors. At the presence near the door they automatically opened, startling Kerry. She wasn't expecting that. She cleared the detectors and headed for the clerks desk and then paused before she got there. "What am I doing?

Trying to give myself a heart attack trying to find out what happened?" Kerry thought to herself. Then she began walking again.

When she got to the desk she asked, "May I please speak with Sheriff Fang?" Kerry was looking at this young, brown haired, brown eyed deputy who she was talking to and thought about asking her if she has ever lost someone dear to her. "no that would be stupid. Stop thinking like this Kerry." She told herself. The young officer had a very sweet, mellow voice when she spoke. "I will call for him. If you will please have a seat, I will let him know that you are here to speak with him." "Thank you very much." Was all Kerry could say without getting all choked up. After waiting approximately five minutes, a tall man with short brown hair, blue eyes and a build of an athlete came through the door. Kerry was very much abridged at the promptness of the station. "May I help you?" Sheriff Fang asked.

"Yes my name is Kerry Benton..." The sheriff cut her off mid-sentence and said, "If you will follow me we can talk in my office. It is more quiet and confidential." "Thank you Mr., I mean Sheriff Fang." Kerry shook her head in in diss-belief at what she had just said. The walk was quite long, but as they walked Sheriff Fang was talking. "Mrs. Benton. Your husband talks very highly of you and the kids. He is a great man." He continued talking but she couldn't really hear because there was too much noise in the building. Upon entering his office, she looked around and saw pictures hanging on the wall of every officer that was killed or injured in the line of duty. As soon as she heard the door close, Kerry burst into tears. "I'm sorry. I just want him to be ok." Kerry said as she sat in a chair. Holding her head with both hands and her elbows perched on both knees. Sheriff Fang offered a tissue box which Kerry took, grateful for the offer. "Mrs. Benton. I know what you are going through. I have lost many loved ones. I have come to think of my crew as my family. I have lost many of them as well. As you can see.

I have to go through this frequently as it happens here as well as to the outside of this family. I am pretty sure that Carl told you, and you see it in the news papers and in the news as well. So I am not telling you anything that you don't already know so far..." He was going to keep talking but he let his words fade fast when he saw that Kerry was looking at him with a questioning look. "I...Can you please tell me what happened?" Kerry asked through sobering sobs.

"Well Mrs. Benton. I only know a little but and will be glad to share tat part with you and then when I find out some more information I will surely let you know also. There was four gunman at Central Station. What was going on there I don't know, but, there was more police force then gunman though. Your husband and a couple other officers pulled up in unit C-809 (K-9), at the wrong time. They pulled up to all the other police vehicles' thinking that it was ok if they hurried. Carl was driving and as soon as one of the shooters had a clear shot he fired, hitting Carl in the leg. Then everyone else started shooting. Officer Palmer, who was his partner, called it in that an officer had been hit and was down. Right after or shortly thereafter she was hit several times in the chest and head. She died on the spot."

Kerry stopped crying and sobered up and said, "I'm gratefully sorry for the loss. Is there anything that I can do to help the family out with anything?" Kerry asked sympathetically. "I will ask and get back to you on that. Everything else is still fuzzy at this point. There was three men wounded, (including Carl) and two men killed." Sheriff Fang paused as if trying to hold back tears of his own. "I'm so very sorry." Kerry is naturally a compassionate person, and she wanted to give him a big hug and comfort him. She didn't though. "In this line of work we put our lives on the line to make it safe for other people. We have lost some good family here throughout the years. We are here to protect." There was a long pause. It was so quiet you could here your own heartbeat in your ears if you paid attention and listened.

Sheriff Fang broke the dead silence when he said, "I almost forgot. A few of the officers put together a basket for you and the other families." He went over to the closet and brought out a big box full of already pre-made dinners, snacks for the kids, little knick-knacks, etc... "Thank you so much to you and to the police family for everything. If there is anything that I can do for the other families, please let me know." "I think you for your kindness and generosity but out family here has it pretty much taken care of." He looked at her with the look of don't give up. "Your kindness is needed elsewhere. Would you like me to take this to your car for you?" "Please. I would be grateful." "I forgot to mention one thing. When we catch the people responsible for all of this, there will be a trial and the victims and family of the victims will be heard. That would be you also Mrs. Benton." Kerry, out of instinct, took the sheriffs hand and thanked him. "Thank you so much for everything. God bless you and your kindness."

At this time Sheriff Fang was looking down at her sympathetically. Kerry saw this and gave him a hug. "You know Mrs. Benton, on a regular basis I would never allow such an act, but considering the circumstances, I believe that this time is appropriate." On the way back to Kim and Bill's house, she couldn't stop thinking of how much hatred had grown to those kids/people who did this to not only Carl but to four other families. She was thinking of a good and just punishment for them. Three-thirty p.m. Kerry was back at Kim and Bill's.

When Kerry pulled up into the driveway, Kim came running out. "So, how did it go? Did you find out who was responsible? Did you get any information?" Kim asked eager to know what was going on. Kerry replied in an amazing calm like manner. "I found out what happened but I didn't find out who has done this. Yes I did find some information and a couple of other things also." Kerry went to the trunk of her car and opened it. She showed Kim what the station had given to them. "Oh, how nice of them. So there was other people hurt also then?" Kerry went inside and sat down with Kim and Bill. She told them everything that Sheriff Fang had told her. Even the joke about already knowing things because of the news and news papers.

Kerry politely told Bill and Kim thanks for watching the kids and that they should really be going to see Carl at the hospital. "Thank you so much for everything guys. I owe you big time." "Honey, you don't owe us anything. Anytime you want to have a little break then please drop them off. We don't mind having them at all. As a matter of fact, we wouldn't mind seeing more of them." Kerry nodded and said, "Thanks again." Tears welled up in Kerry's eyes as she saw the kindness that was coming forth to her family. Kim and Bill both embraced Kerry, showing her love and compassion. Then they prayed with Kerry, Hailley and Jacob before they left to go back to the hospital. Bill asked Kerry, "After you have spent some time with Carl boy, then please call us so we can go see him also ok?"

Kerry looked up at Bill and said, "Bill. You and Kim are the first people I came to. You know that I would for sure let you know. Thanks again guys." Kerry got the kids in the car and started back towards the hospital.

Chapter Two

THE TRANSFUSION

At the hospital where Carl was sleeping, or so the nurse thought that he was. The doctors and the burses were talking in his room about his condition. "He needs a blood transfusion. He has lost a lot of blood and he might not make it if he doesn't get it." Dr. Curtis was saying to the nurses. "What type of blood do we need and I will go get it." Stated one of the nurses. Carl could tell that this nurse was young, and might be pretty new at the job. He could tell by the shakiness in her voice. "He is AB+ and he will need two." "I will be right back." Said the young nurse. In the mean time, the doctor and one of the other nurses were checking on him. The nurse checked his usual vitals and the doctor was checking his fluids and documenting everything in his chart. When the doctor and nurse were finished and documented everything that needed to be, they left Carl's room and let him sleep. The young nurse came back into the room and was getting ready to put the I.V. for the blood into his arm. She cleaned the area and then sterilized it with sanitation wipes and things. When she was ready to put the I.V. in his arm Carl flinched, which made the nurse even more nervous and pause.

Not noticing the Carl had his eyes open and was looking at her, she tried again. This time Carl reached over and softly grabbed her wrist. The young nurse was startled. Carl softly said, "I didn't mean to startle you, but before anything happens, I would really like my wife's consent also. That is after I tell her everything that was said so that way she knows and is updates as much as I am.? Carl said with cotton mouth, and then added "I would also like some water...If that is not too much to ask." Carl said looking into the nurses eyes who was staring back at him with fear in them. "I...I will have to speak with Dr. Curtis first sir." "Thank you very much."

After Carl said thank you he gently released the nurses wrist. The nurse left the room in a swift haste. Carl laid there with his eyes shut until he heard someone walk in. "I really hope that you brought that water because I am so thirsty, my mouth couldn't get any dryer."

Carl said without opening his eyes. There was no reply. There was Kerry, looking down on him, tears streaming down her cheeks. A single tear rolled down her cheek and over her chin. That single tear ended up dripping off and landing on Carl's hand. Carl opened his eyes to Kerry leaning down and looking at him face to face.

"There you are my beautiful bride. I thought that you would have been here a lot sooner than this." Carl said reaching a hand up and wiping the tears from her cheeks. Kerry couldn't find any words to say. Kerry leaned down and gave him an ever so soft kiss. "I love you. I would have been here a long time ago, but the doctor said that you needed your rest. So I went to the police station after dropping the kids off at Kim and Bill's. I talked with your boss. Very nice gentlemen. The police station gave us a box of food that I don't have to cook, just warm up. After I got done there I went and got the kids and took them out to eat. We case straight here after that. I got the call that you were here around eight-thirty a.m. and got here at nine-fifteen a.m. Kerry said without lifting her eyes from Carl.

Hailley came up and said hello to her dad. "hey Robocop. How are you feeling?" Carl had a smile on his face and in a like manor said, "I am as good as could be, but I wish that I was home. Guess you guys got out of school today eh?" Carl asked. "Yeah, we spent the day at Aunt Kim and Uncle Bill's house." "Hi daddy." Jacob said as he came up. Kerry grabbed him before he could pounce on Carl like usual. "Hey tiger. How are ya?" "Daddy. When are you coming home?" "I don't know tiger." "Hailley. Why don't you take Jacob and go see the babies. I would like to speak with your father." Hailley nodded and walked out with Jacob's hand in hers. "The doctor told me that I would need a blood transfusion of I wanted to live much longer. Well, didn't really tell me, but the nurses. I just over heard."

"Well, have they started it yet?" Kerry asked. Carl simply pointed to the blood bags that were hanging on the I.V. pole. "No they haven't. I told them that I wanted to speak with you before they do anything to me." "Carl, honey, if it is going to save your life then why not let them do it." Kerry explained. "Kerry. I would like to, but I told them you would have to consent to it. Plus, I want to make sure that I really need it before they do it." Kerry nodded in agreement. Pushing the button for the nurse to come in, as Dr. Curtis arrived. "Well, well, well. Look who is up. Have you reached an agreement on the transfusion yet?" Dr. Curtis asked while standing on the side of Carl's bed. Kerry asked. "I would like to make sure that he really needs the blood before proceeding please." "Mam. We already did the tests and it shows that he needs it."

"Well, will you please run them again?" Kerry asked. Carl looked at the doctor and nodded in agreement to what Kerry was asking for. Dr. Curtis ran the tests again and the whole time Kerry and Carl were praying that the Lord's hand to be on this situation and that God would deal with this accordingly. "I don't know how this is going to change anything. It has been an hour and he might need more now." Dr. Curtis said. "Dr. Curtis. You are needed at the lab at once. Dr. Curtis STAT." The doctor ran out and left the nurses to do vitals and check fluids on Carl. "Whatever happens we know that this is what God had in store, and how the good Lord has answered us." Carl said. "Yes my love. We just have to keep praying, trusting God and having complete and total faith that this is God." Kerry said.

"You know. I would have thought that you would have handled this a lot worse but you are handling it very well." Carl said looking up at Kerry who was still holding his hand and standing by his side. "Thank you dear, but we are not in the clear yet. I could still get rational you know." Kerry said with a twinkle in her eye, from the tears that were still coming. At that moment Dr. Curtis along with three nurses came in and had a bewildered look on their faces. "What is it? What is wrong?" Kerry asked thinking the worst but hoping for the better. "I don't know how, and I don't know why, but your blood shows that your are good to go and the transfusion is no longer needed. I would like to keep you here for a few more days to make sure that everything is going to be ok."

Kerry grabbed Carl and hugged him tightly, forgetting about his shoulder. "Ooo, honey, please be careful. Still hurts you know." Carl said. Kerry looked the doctor straight in the eyes and said, "You know as well as we do that the reason that he doesn't need the blood is because of God. This is all because of God. This shows how quickly God can work medicals." Tears streaming down Kerry's cheeks uncontrollably now. Carl looked at the doctor and said, "Is this enough proof for you to want to know God as your Lord and Savior now?" "I...I am speechless." Dr. Curtis said. The nurses left the room, but Dr. Curtis stayed behind and talked with Kerry and Carl some more about faith and trusting God's hand and power. A few hours later Hailley and Jacob came back into the room. "You should have seen the babies mom. They were so cute. Can we take one home?" Jacob asked.

"No dear. Those babies belong to other proud mommies and daddies. See how happy you are Jacob dear?" Kerry asked. "Yes mommy." "That is how happy you and Hailley made mommy and daddy when you were born." Kerry said. "We are truly blessed to have you guys." Carl added. Kerry and the kids stayed with Carl for another few hours and then went home for the night. "Carl, honey. If you need me tonight, will you please call me? I will be back tomorrow ok." Kerry said tears welling up in her eyes again. "Yes Kerry. I will do that. I will be here. Don't you worry about me going anywhere. I love you Kerry and I love you my little rascals'. Take good care of mommy ok?" "We love you to daddy and we will."

With that being said Kerry leaned down and gave Carl a kiss before leaving. When Kerry and the kids got to the car, Kerry called Kim and Bill and asked if thy could tae the kids for a couple of days. "Kerry. You don't have to ask us. Just bring them over ok. You know that. Even if I'm at work Kim will be here. She is good with the children's and treats them like her own. We love you and the kids Kerry and we will do as much as we can to help." Bill said. "I know. Thank you so very much for everything. I love you guys and I know that the kids do to.." Kerry said through sobering sobs. "I will be dropping them off within the hour. Thanks again." "We will be awaiting their arrival. It is our pleasure."

When Kerry dropped Hailley and Jacob off, Kim invited her to stay for dinner and relax some. "I would love to." Kerry said. After dinner, later that night Kerry went home. Kerry had a hard time sleeping that night knowing Carl's condition and that the kids might be having a hard time dealing with this and just not being able to express it to Kerry. "Too many thought and concerns to be able to sleep. It is now four a.m. and I have yet to go to sleep. I am going to go spend some time with Carl." Kerry told herself. When Kerry went out to her car, waiting for it to warm up. She noticed that the neighbor, Mr. Kline, was watching her through the window. She hurriedly left the house and got to the hospital as fast as she possibly could.

While driving to the hospital she told herself that she wasn't going to tell Carl about this yet. He doesn't need to worry about it just yet. He has bigger things to worry about. Like his health. On the drive, after telling herself that, she turned on the radio and it was spirit 105.3 F.M. It gave the number to call and so she did. She talked to someone live on air and asked for prayer for Carl. They prayed with her. They also sent her a book and a bunch of other things. When she got off the phone with Spirit 105.3, she called the pastor and told him. "Is he stable now? How is he doing?" Pastor Gregg asked. "He is doing better. Been praying a lot for him." "I bet you have. Can he have visitors yet?' "I don't know. That is something that you will have to call the hospital and find out."

"Well thank for letting us know. We have been and will continue to pray for him in church." "Thank you." Said Kerry. When Kerry got t the hospital, she prayed for good health for Carl and that healing would come quick. As she stood at the foot of his bed, she cried all the tears that she possibly could cry. She cried herself to sleep. When Carl woke up in the morning Kerry's head was on his bed. She was holding his hand and she was fast asleep. Carl looked at her and prayed for Kerry. Dr. Curtis came by to check on Carl and see how he was doing when he saw Kerry asleep. He tried to be as quiet as he possibly could. "Long night for her I take it huh?" Dr. Curtis said. "Yeah. I think that this is taking as much out of her as it is with me." Carl said trying to make a joke.

By ten a.m., Pastor Gregg had called the hospital to check on Carl and see if he could have visitors yet. "I am calling on behalf of Carlos Benton. I am Pastor Gregg. I was wondering if he could have a couple visitors this morning?" "I think that his wife is in there and at this time he is only allowed two visitors at a time. We try to visit the visitors for the patients sake. Less germs the better the patient recovers and the faster." Said the young polite nurse. "You are more than welcome to come though." "Thank you and we do understand what you are saying." Pastor Gregg said. Around one p.m. Kerry woke up. She heard people talking and realized that Carl was up talking to Pastor Gregg who arrived. "Well good morning love. How did you sleep?" "I slept great." Kerry said. "HI Pastor Gregg. I am glad that you came by because I think that it is good for Carl here to have some other company than just his wife."

Chapter 3

THE HOME COMING

"It is ok. I wanted to see him anyway. I am on my way to a meeting and the hospital was on my way there. So I figured I would stop by and say hello." Pastor Gregg said. "I am going to get something to eat and let Bill and Kim come and see you. Is that ok with you Carl?" Kerry asked. "Yes dear." Carl said. Kerry went over to Kim and Bill's house and told them that they could go see Carl now and that she would stay with the kids. "Thanks Kerry. I really wanted to see Carl boy. How does he look today?" Asked Bill. "He looks great. Surprisingly enough he was actually sitting up." "Wow. Good for him. Pretty soon they will have him walking." Bill said with a little laugh. By five p.m. Bill and Kim were at the hospital, standing beside Carl's bed. "Hey Carl ol' boy. How ya doin?" Bill said. "Heard they were going to have you up and walking soon." Bill said with a laugh. "Hey there roger rabbit. Heard you were watching the little rascals'? Have they been good for you guys?" "Yes they have been. It has also been very nice to actually be able to spend some good quality time with them. They are sure good kids." Kim answered for Bill. "Yeah. Thanks for letting us have them." Bill replied. "Good. I'm glad to hear it. Thanks for taking them." Carl said. "So when is the big tournament?" Carl asked. "Oh. That's next week. Little Jacob sure wants to go." Bill stated. "Well I'm not so sure that we are going to be able to afford it. You know after this happy family reunion." Carl answered.

"If you know what I mean because now we are going to have so many expensive bills you know." Carl added. "Hey, Carl boy. First is this. If you wanted us all to be together, all you had to do is just cal. Secondly, no worries, if you say that he can come the I will pay for the ticket for him." Bill said. "Oh. I don't know. I would have to talk with the wife first." "Sounds good t me." Bill said. "Hey Bill. We are supposed to be asking how Carl is you know." Kim stated. "Oh yeah. Thanks dear for reminding me." "So when did they say that you would be going home? Or do you know?" Kim asked. "They said sometime soon. Hopefully within in the next couple of days." Carl replied back with high hopes. "Well that's good!" Bill and Kim said in unison. Everyone laughed. Meanwhile, back at Kim and Bill's house where Kerry and the kids were, something was going on. Kerry told the kids that she would like to do something nice for them. So the kids helped clean the house and get a romantic dinner made so when they got home, they would enjoy a nice warm dinner and a clean house. All the while Kerry was spending some good time with the kids.

Kerry calls Kim's cell and asked when they will be back home. Kim said, "I don't know Bill is really ademit about making sure that Carl is going to be ok. I keep telling him that you will be back and that is what the nurses and doctors are her for." "Can I talk to Bill please?" Kerry asked. "Yeah, hang on and I will get him." "Hello..." Bill said to Kerry. "And how are you and the kids doing?" Bill asked. "Quite good actually. I was hoping to know when you would be home? The reason that I ask is because the kids and I have something for you but we need to know what time you are going to be home to give it to you." Kerry said with eager excitement in her voice. "Well Kerry. That is difficult to say because we were going to go out for dinner afterwards." Bill said with a little regret in his voice.

"Bill, honestly. I think that you should just come back and get some rest. You have had a long, tough couple of days." Kerry said with a little remorse in her tone. "Yeah Kerry. You might be right. We should be home around eight o'clock. If that is ok?" "Yeah, that's fine. Thanks Bill for letting me know and drive safe." Kerry said more relaxed now. "Your welcome sis." "Oh Bill..." Kerry said hoping to catch him before he hung the phone up. "Yeah!" "How is Carl doing?" "Well, he seems to think that he is going home in a couple of days." "Yeah. That is what the doctor said." "He looks good, but, he has the chills and I'm trying to get the doctor to tell me or give Carl some sort of something to help warm him up." Bill said. "Carl is strong. Please just keep me posted ok?" Kerry asked.

"Sure thing Kerry." Bill said before hanging up the phone with her. "So Carl. That was Kerry asking how you were and if there was something she could do for you." "I know. She is too concerned with me and needs to relax a little bit." Carl said. "Carl. She has the right to be concerned. I mean you are her husband and you have been in this place for what, a week now?" "No. I have been here for three days." Carl corrected Bill. "Kim before I forget. I told Kerry that we would be home by eight o'clock. We need to leave soon if we are going to be there on time. Kerry needs to rest some to. I am thinking that she needs to leave the kids with us tonight and get some rest of her own." "Yeah. That sounds great. Lets go. Carl, she will be up here soon ok? We are going to watch the kids tonight so she can get some rest and if she is going to come up here then it can just be the two of you." Kim said bending down to kiss Carl on the forehead.

"later buddy. Take it easy. Don't go anywhere." Bill said and then shook Carl's hand.

Carl looked at him and then pulled him close trying to keep quiet. "I will meet you in the hallway dear." Bill said to Kim. "Ok." "Do me a favor..." As soon as the door closed Carl started talking again. "Please keep an eye on the kids and Kerry for me. She is going through a lot and I know that she is stressing." Carl asked through red, teary eyes. "Of course bud. You know I will. She is my little sister. I would do anything for her, the kids and you." Bill said back and squeezed his hand and walked out. As Bill was walking out Carl said thanks. "Thanks Bill, for everything." Bill turns around and looks Carl dead in the eyes and said, "Carl you don't have to thank me. You know that you don't because I don't mind at all. Your welcome though." Meanwhile Kerry and the kids fixed a really fancy dinner, lit candles and cleaned the house.

When Kim and Bill got home, they noticed that all the lights were off. They thought that Kerry and the kids might have fallen asleep. "Bill, honey. We should let them stay the night. Kerry must be exhausted." "Yeah, your right." Bill got out of the car and went around and let Kim out. Bill unlocked the door and found a note that was taped to the door that read.

"Please do not be alarmed. We did not leave. Just thought that it would be nice to do something nice for you.

God bless,

Kerry, Hailley and Jacob.

Kim and Bill went in, put their coats away and then saw a fancy dinner under candle light. They sat down and prayed over their meal. "Thank you precious Father for giving us a lovely family. Thank you for protecting Carl and keeping him safe. Thank you Father for giving him another chance at life. Thank you for the wonderful dinner that was prepared for us and provided for us by your loving hands. Amen."

After they ate dinner Kerry told Bill and Kim that she would be going back to the hospital to be with Carl. "Thank you Kerry for cleaning the house and making the wonderful dinner. It was very good and the house looks fantastic." "You are more then welcome. It was the least that I could have done to say thank you for all of your help."

"Kerry. You don't have to thank us. That is what families are all about. Helping other family members out when needed and to love as God loves us. You are welcome though." Kim said as she held Kerry in her arms trying to console her. "Kim. I was always taught to be ever so grateful for what is given to you because you never know when the last time something will be given to you. I thank God every day for all of my blessings. I even thank him for all my trials because I know that God will never put anything in my path that I'm unable to handle. Plus it just makes us stronger and our faith and trust in God grow. Although, I also know that sometimes it is not God who puts it in out path but the devil.

God allows it to happen though for the exact reason as to why I thank him for my trials." Kerry stated as she pulled gently away from Kim so she was arms length away still able to hold her shoulders.

"Wow Kerry. Your faith and trust in God is strong. I thank God for that. I have never really thought of it in that way that you have just said. Thank you so much for opening my eyes to a new kind of light in which I will have to try now." Kim said with an astonished yet bewildered look on her face. "Just to let you know that not everyone can do this. It is actually called the gift of thanks. Some people have it and then some people don't. So do us all a favor and don't get discouraged if you try it and it just doesn't seem to be working out for you." Kerry said trying o explain it to Kim without hurting her feelings. "Ok. I will try not to. Thank you so much for the words of encouragement. It really means a lot to me." Kim said to Kerry with a twinkle of a tear coming out. "Well off I go to be with Carl." Kerry said exhausted from stress, worry and undoubtedly no sleep. "Hey Kerry. One thing that you have to remember is DON'T WORRY!"

Kim said to Kerry as she was getting into her car. Kerry looked up at Kim and stated, "How am I not going to worry, and why did you say that?" Kerry asked kind of bewildered because of the timing. What Kim had said came completely out of the blue. "Well Kerry. It is an old saying that worrying is like a rocking chair. It gets you nowhere but back and forth. Instead I know you and I know how strong your faith and trust in God is and if that is the case then you need to just lay all of it down at the foot of the cross and let God deal according to this as it is in his will because if it is in God's will, NOTHING and I mean nothing can and will ever change it. Just think about that. Now with that being said, goodnight, thanks again and drive safely. Last but not least, love ya'." Kim said still having her hands on the window block of the car, slowly easing to a standing position to let Kerry drive away. "Thanks Kim. I will ponder that thought and pray about what you said." When Kerry reached the hospital, visiting hours were over, but the nurse let Kerry into Carl's private room anyways. Upon walking into Carl's room, Kerry found Carl fast asleep, in a sitting up position.

Kerry wanted ever so badly to walk over and lay his bed down for him so he wouldn't wake up with a sore back or anything in the morning. She sopped and just studied Carl from the door. Kerry stood there just admiring God's gift for a good hour while he slept. After an hour of watching Carl sleep ever so soundly, she noticed he stirred and woke up. When Carl looked, he saw Kerry standing there and he asked, "How long have you been standing there?" "Well. I walked in about an hour ago and saw you sleeping so soundlessly. Even though I wanted to put the head of your bed down for you, but, knowing that I wasn't able to do that without disturbing yours sleep and rest that you undoubtedly need. I decided to stand her and gaze and admire God's gift of a good man of God you are." Kerry said now sitting on the side of his bed, holding his left hand in both of hers and looking with longing eyes into his. "Well dear. It looks as if tomorrow we will 100% know if I am and when I will be going home." Carl said as excited as he could get.

"Well we will have to see and wait until tomorrow honey. Do me a favor and don't get your hopes up, ok love? I don't like to see you disappointed." Kerry said holding back excitement herself. "Yes dear. Now you need to get some well deserved rest." Carl said looking at Kerry. "Yes dear. So do you. I will lay next to you, so we both get a good night sleep. I love you." Kerry said, looking into Carl's eyes, with her left hand n Carl's right cheek, leaning into a kiss. "I love you to dear." Carl said as he kissed Kerry, ever so softly as the night when he left Kerry and was shot. The next morning bright and early Carl rose with the sun and laid there and watched Kerry sleeping ever so sweetly in his arms.

The doctor came into Carl's room at a quarter to eight and told him he had some good news and some bad news to tell him. Carl simply looked up at Dr. Curtis and said, "I really don't want to hear any news right now, good or bad. I really want, and all I want right now to do is spend quality time watching my wife sleep so soundlessly and pray. So if you could wait until she wakes up so she could hear the news with me, I would be ever so grateful. Thanks." Carl said looking up at the doctor with pleading eyes to wait. "Yes. I will respect that of you. Is there anything else that my staff can do for you as you and all of us wait?" Dr. Curtis asked Carl before walking out the door. "Well, if it is not too much, may I have a nice, good cup of coffee?" Carl asked ever so quietly. "Yes sir. We will bring it to you soon."

Dr. Curtis said. Eight O'clock a.m. Kerry stirs and rolls to her right side. Opens her eyes and looks up at Carl with questioning eyes. "Did you get enough sleep my dear?" Kerry asked Carl. "yes dear. I did. I was just enjoying you laying next to me and being able to watch you sleep once again is ever so nice. I just hope that today, the news that the Dr. has for us is to tell us that it will be this week sometime." Carl said looking at Kerry. Bending his neck to give her a kiss, the Dr. came back in and asked if now was a good time. "Well Dr. Curtis. Now is as good a time as any." Kerry looked a little worried and then upon remembering what Kim had told her she somewhat relaxed.

Dr. Curtis pulled up a chair and was now sitting beside Carl. "I know that you were really looking forward to going home soon, and you will be going home, if all goes well and nothing shows up in your blood and every test comes back good. Ok?" Dr. Curtis said. Carl looked at the doctor and asked, "Well you said that you had some good and bad news for us. So I take it that is the good news? So what is the bad news if you may please?" Carl asked upon glancing at Kerry to see what her reaction would be. "Yes Carl, sir. That would have been the good news and now the bad news is. Is that that you will have to have a phlebotomist coming to your house one-three times a week to draw your blood and give your steroid shots." Dr. Curtis said, switching his gaze from Carl to Kerry, back and forth.

Carl looked at Kerry and said, "Well at least at this time it is good news and really no bad news." Kerry looked at Carl with a shy gleam in her eyes as if she was going to cry or something. "Kerry honey, what is it? Are you ok?" Carl looked at Kerry and his facial expressions changed from a glee look to more of a concerned look. "No Carl. I'm good. Just wore out and know Jacob is going to be going to that ttournament with Bill remember? I am just hoping that doesn't fall on the same day as you coming home. Well what we could do is wait until this evening, and then ask the doctor exactly when you will be going home. Then call everyone and let them know." Kerry said, eyes still red and stinging from being overly tired still. "Get some more sleep darling. We will talk more about it after you get some more rest."

Carl replied putting his arm a little more snug around Kerry to make her feel a little more comforted. "Yes dear." Was all Kerry could find herself to say before falling back to sleep so fast. Half past eleven a.m. Kerry wakes back up to find Carl up and sitting in the reclining chair watching Kerry sleep and reading the Bible. :honey. Where did you get the Bible from?" Kerry asked Carl getting to a sitting position on the side of the bed. Pastor Gregg brought it when he came by. I think that he was going to use it at the conference that night, but, he must have forgotten it. Pretty sure that he has another Bible though. Yes I will be returning it to him this Sunday." Carl said looking up at Kerry who by now, had bed head. "Oh ok dear. Do you want to talk to the doctor now if he is available to do so?" Kerry asked Carl.

"Yes. I would like to pray first though if we may." Carl said putting a small piece of paper off the bedside table to mark his spot, not to lose it. "Yes dear please do. We also have to remember that because we pray for healing and fast recovery in here, does NOT mean that it all stops as soon as you get home. We have to remember that all glory goes to God, because without his loving arms of protection then I strongly believe that you would not be with us today. So all honor and glory goes to God." Kerry said looking at Carl, and getting the feeling he was going to give a very smart remark in return, but didn't. Carl simply grabbed Kerry's hands in his and started in on prayer.

"Precious, Heavenly Father. Kerry and I come to you, humbly asking that not ours but your will be done. May we through the strength shown, give you glory for what you have done thus far, and what you are so graciously going to do now and forever more according to your will. Let nothing that Kerry or I do be according to anyone's will but yours. Let your light and love shine every so brightly so that others see how happy we are, and come to us and ask why we look like we're glowing, but, it is all your radiant glow through us Father. Right then and there we can whiteness to others about you because they came to us and asked us about you. Father, God, right now we come to you giving your name, and you God, all the glory and honor for what you have done thus far. For the fast and speedy recovery and the transfusion that was no longer needed.

Father, God. Thank you for touching my body in ways that even has the Doctors, nurses and specialist wondering and puzzled and mind boggled. We have the one and only answer, and that answer is you God. You are the answer to why I'm healed. you are the only explanation as to why I'm still here, why the transfusion is no longer needed and why I'm healing so fast God. We give you thanks because without our faith and 100% trust, this would not be possible. Because of you, you are opening doors for us to not only be lights of your world, but to openly share your word and help people come to know you. Let them see the outlook that we see and how the world around them is and how all the sin and the every day living is one large temptation Father.

We also come to you humbly asking that this doesn't stop when I go home Father, but, rather gets bigger and stronger and everything goes exactly how you have had this planned. The way your will is all planned out God. Please don't ever let our light dim, flash or even weaken for even a split second Father. God let our lights grow and get bigger and brighter so that people can see from miles and miles away Father God. Thanks be to God who gives us the wisdom and knowledge as to what to say and the things we do and places we go. We pray all and everything in your name, Amen."

"Thank you Carl for praying. That was very beautiful and yes God listened and is answering. Now all we have to do is listen. Now let us call Dr. Curtis in and see what he has to tell us." Kerry said look at Carl with a tears stained cheek from his prayer. "Lets." Replied Carl. one O'clock p.m. Dr. Curtis comes in. This time no nurses and he closes the door behind him. Something that Dr. Curtis has ever done since Carl has been his patient. "Remember when I came in here. One of the very first times and told you about your blood test coming back, then you asked me to run them again. You prayed and then you told me about God and you asked me if it was enough proof to want to get to know God as my personal Lord and Savior?" The doctor looked up at Carl and Kerry after finishing that sentence with tears coming out of both eyes, not just one. "Yes doc. I do remember that day. We have prayed and prayed, not only for you, but for others as well to come to know God." Carl said trying not to let tears come out of his eyes because of the prayer he had just prayed and then now this. "wow. God answers quickly and how slow some are to hear his voice, but this time is loud and clear." Kerry said looking directly at the doctor now who was red faced from crying now. He now laid the tablet and pen on Carl's bed to talk more. "Well. I have given much ad deep thought to what you have said and visually seeing your speedy recovery. I can honestly say that I have faith and want to know God as my Lord and Savior and humbly ask him to come rejuvenate my life to make me whole again."

Dr. Curtis said, almost crying, and shaking uncontrollably now. "Yes. Praise God. Thank you Jesus for your answer to prayers. Praise God." Kerry and Carl both said kind of startling the Doctor, just a little bit. He went along with it just fine though. "So I'm asking if you would help me and walk me through this?" Dr. Curtis asked gently. "With all our hearts. We would be honored to help and take the first baby steps with you. Just to let you know though that it will be baby steps and will take time. Honestly you never really fully learn everything. Truly I'm still learning myself. Remember, baby steps. Don't forget, when you don't understand something refer back to the Bible. You can also always call Kerry and I and we would be glad to help you also. We will be here for you where ever you need us and will help you as much as possible. You will also need to find a great home church though. That will also help tremendously.

Carl said taking the doctors hand in has right hand and Kerry's in his left, hoping not to offend the doctor. "We will pray now so that way it is the first steps to the rest of your life." Kerry said. "Please repeat after me if you may." Carl said looking at Dr. Curtis. Dr. Curtis just nodded in agreement. "Lord, we all come to you right now giving thanks for letting another child come to know you and want to come to know you. Thank you for letting your light shine so brightly. Lord, I come to you to ask a question." Carl said. "Lord, I come to you to ask a question." The Doctor repeated after Carl. Kerry gripped Carl's hand in excitement. "Lord, I humbly ask that you come into my life and make me a new man." Carl said. "Lord, I humbly ask that you come into my life and make me a new man." Dr. Curtis repeated. "I humbly ask that you be my Lord and Savior and rule and reign over my life and forgive me for all my sins Lord, God."

Carl said and the doctor repeats. "I humbly ask that you be my Lord and Savior and rule and reign over my life and forgive me for all my sins Lord, God." "I ask that you be my personal Lord and Savior and guide me, and be the lamp unto my feet and the light unto my path." Carl said. "I ask that you be my personal Lord and Savior and guide me, and be the lamp unto my feet and the light unto my path." Dr. Curtis repeated. "Thank you God for your undying and unconditional love." Carl said and Dr. Curtis repeated. "Thank you God for you undying and unconditional love." "We pray these things in your precious and most holy name." Carl said. All in agreement "AMEN." "Thank you Lord for giving the gift of eternal life to our dear brother Dr. Curtis. Thank you for his salvation." Kerry said.

"I have some more good news for you both. Um, it looks like you will be able to go home tomorrow." Dr. Curtis said. Kerry and Carl both just looked at each other and then hugged and gave each other a loving kiss. "Well. With that being said I will be getting your papers ready for you and letting you know all orders and n home Dr. phone numbers and everything you will need." Dr. Curtis stated and walked out with a new shining light radiating from his new found faith. "Kerry will you call and tell everyone about this because I need to take a shower?" Carl asked Kerry. "Well dear. I think that people would be more please to hear about it and more happy about it if it came from you." Kerry said with a glee gleam in her eyes. "Yes. I think that you might be right. I will do it when I get out of the shower. Thank you so much for loving me and staying by my side.. I love you." Carl said. "I love you to and your welcome even though you don't have to thank me for doing my wifely duties." Kerry said.

Chapter 4

FIRST DAYS HOME

At four O'clock p.m. Carl took a long, well deserved, as hot as hospital water can get, shower. While Carl was in the shower, Kerry sat on the recliner chair and prayed hard. All the while thanking God for her new found faith of her new brother and the good news about Carl's getting to go home. When Carl got out of the shower he saw Kerry sitting in the recliner, hands folded and head bowed with a couple drops of blood on the floor were her head was bowed. He quickly went to her aide. He put both hands on her shoulders and made her look at him. Upon looking up into Carl's eyes, he could tell that she was being touched by the Holy Spirit and laid her back so she didn't fall. The blood that Carl saw was coming from her nose. The intensity of the Holy Spirit moving within her was powerful.

Powerful enough to make her nose bleed and go into a very deep trans. Not knowing how long this one would last, he sat on the edge of the hospital bed and prayed also. Not only thanking God but praying for Kerry. When Kerry came to, she got cleaned up and laid down n Carl's bed ad listened while he as calling everyone to tell them not only about his home coming, but, also about their new brother in Christ. When Carl called Kim and Bill to tell them Bill said, "Good for you. I'm happy to hear about our new brother in Christ our Lord. So did they give you an exact time, or is that still uncertain yet?" Bill asked. "Well, they are not able to give exact times for anything, but, he did say sometime before noon. So that is a blessing all in itself." Carl stated back.

"Yes brother it is. We will be happy to keep the kids a few extra days, knowing that I am going to be taking Jacob to that tournaments in the next couple of days anyways. So really. It is no problem at all. Is there anything else we can do for you to help this go smooth?" Bill asked excitedly. "No. You and Kim have done enough. Just for having the kids so we don't have to worry about them. God has blessed us in ways we can not even begin to have enough thanks for. Don't get me wrong. We have been thanking him for everything. Even the little things." Carl stated. Bill replied with, "Carl. Nothing that you have to be thankful for has been small or little. More or less, everything has been huge and that is that. So it is anything but little. I'm sure that all the thanks that you guys are doing is enough to God. He knows your hearts and everything in between. So just keep doing what your doing."

"Well, I know. Thanks for that reminder. Kerry and I do know that. Well bro, I better get off the phone and get some rest now. Love ya' and thanks again." Carl said. "No problem. Love ya' to. Bye." Bill said and hung up the phone. Upon hanging the phone up, Carl glanced over at Kerry who was now asleep with a smile across her face. Carl slowly got up and quietly walked over to the bed and laid next to Kerry, put his right arm around her, told her he loved her and then kissed her forehead. Then Carl fell asleep. Kerry and Carl were both so tired that they slept through dinner and onto the next morning. At three a.m. Kerry got up. A nurse came into the room to check on Carl and do some vitals. Kerry asked very politely if she could get a cup of coffee. "Yes mam. I will bring it to you as soon as I am done here with Carl." The nurse said politely.

Upon returning with her coffee, Kerry asked the nurse, "Do you have any idea how happy we are about him getting to go home, and how fast God works wonders?" When she asked the nurse this she just stood there. Almost like she couldn't believe that this lady could speak so openly, and without fear of God or being prosecuted for it. "Yes mam. I do." Replied the nurse. Kerry then asked, "How are his vitals and blood work looking?' The nurse replied still aw struck. "Well, we are just nurses. The doctor will have to come talk to you about his blood. His vitals look really good though. He seems to be more relaxed. Almost like a big burden has been lifted." "Yes mam. I have noticed that also. Thank you so much. Thank you for the coffee also."

"Your welcome." The nurse replied. Then the nurse was gone. Kerry had a warm sensation running through her veins as she was speaking with the nurse. Kerry sat in the recliner and was watching Carl sleep. Dr. Curtis came into the room. He was dressed in street clothes so Kerry barely recognized him. He pulled the doctor stool out and had a seat. He was talking to Kerry and told her that Carl would be released right after breakfast, and that his vitals and blood work all looked extremely well. "Kerry. I've done some praying and thinking. Is it ok with you, because it is my day off, if I was here for his release?" The doctor asked as if he wanted to tell her what he had gotten for them as a going home, get well soon gift. Kerry looked at Dr. Curtis and said, "I think that Carl would really like that."

At nine a.m. Carl, Dr. Curtis ad Kerry was all sitting around talking, laughing and drinking coffee while enjoying each others company. Nine-ten a.m. a new nurse walked in with discharge papers for Carl. When Carl had them in his hand, he never saw this particular nurse before, but it was the same nurse that was Kerry was talking to earlier. Carl looked up at her and Dr. Curtis asked her, "I've never seen you before. Are you a newbie?" "Yes sir. As a matter of fact I am. To this part of it. My first day." "Well, welcome aboard. I'm just so sorry that you really didn't get to talk and get to know Kerry and Carl. They are very good people. What is your name mam?" Dr. Curtis asked the young nurse. "My name is Faith…" Upon telling them her name she started radiating light, like a beam of light from heaven was shining on her and made her shine as she finished talking.

"God sent me to tell Carl and Kerry that because of their faith in Him and their undying love for God, He has healed and proved He is God. Through His power and love, Carl was healed so that you Brian Daniel Curtis, would come to know Christ and have everlasting life and enter the streets of gold through the pearly white gates of heaven. God loves you and wants you to do more good things. He has one more task at hand for you, Carl. It isn't going to be easy." The nurse stated, took the papers from Carl that he had signed and walked off. Nine-thirty a.m. a different nurse came in to give Carl his copies of his discharge papers. "Well. I guess this is good-bye." Dr. Curtis said. "I do have a couple gifts for you guys though." "Good-bye?!" Kerry and Carl said in unison. "No. You are more then welcome to come with us to the house and visit for a while if you would like." Carl stated.

"Yeah and intrude on your first day home? I think that I will be ok. I will just tell the driver to follow you." Dr. Curtis said. "We insist Dr. Curtis. After everything you have done for us, it is the least that we can do." Kerry said. "Ok, well if you put it that way. I guess that I can swing by for a few and help out." Dr. Curtis said and then reached over and shook Carl and Kerry's hand. "I'll follow you then." Dr. Curtis stated while walking off. when getting to the driveway to the house, Carl told Kerry to pull into the garage and tell Dr. Curtis and the driver to pull into the yard. "Ok, Carl. Will do." Kerry told Carl she would be right back and went to tell Dr. Curtis and the driver what Carl had told her to tell them. As Kerry was walking back to help Carl she noticed that the driver had a medical truck.

"You know Carl. Dr. Curtis has been very nice and he has a big medical truck also. He really didn't have to get us anything." Kerry told Carl. "Yes dear. I know that. Do you remember how God laid it on our hearts to give that one family in need a couple hundred dollars so they could actually get food and diapers and clothes and shoes for their children? Well maybe God has laid it on his heart to give to us. Almost like a pay it forward type ordeal." Carl replied back to Kerry. "Yes dear. Maybe your right. We should just be thankful." Kerry said. "Yes dear." Replied Carl. They all met at the front door and entered the house. Even the driver of the truck. When they all got inside Dr. Curtis asked where Carl would be sleeping. "In the spare bedroom for now until I can get up the stairs again." Said Carl.

"Ok well, I was going to put your new bed in there if you don't mind?" Stated Dr. Curtis. "Yes. That will work just fine. Thank you." Said Carl. Dr. Curtis went out to his car and got his briefcase and then came back in. When Dr. Curtis came back in he saw Kerry and Carl sitting on the couch together in the family room. "How do you feel Carl?" Asked Dr. Curtis. "Oh fine. Just a little tired, but good overall. Thanks for asking." Carl said. "My pleasure." Dr. Curtis stated while digging through his briefcase trying to find something. "Does anyone want anything to drink?" Kerry asked. "I'll take some water please." Said the driver. "I'll have some coffee, black please." Said Dr. Curtis. "For you dear. What would you like?" "I'll have some sweet tea please." With that Kerry disappeared into the kitchen.

While Kerry was busy in the kitchen, getting everyone's drinks, Carl asked Dr. Curtis why he did it. "Well. I honestly don't know Carl. I just felt like I had to." Dr. Curtis answered. "you do realize that when you get the feeling, usually God is the one who is laying it on your heart to do so. Sometimes he tells you to do something. When he tells you to do something, you better do it." Carl stated, and then they both laughed. Kerry came back into the room with water for the driver, coffee for Dr. Curtis and sweet tea for Carl. "I got myself a cafe late." Said Kerry. Dr. Curtis pulled out a card and his checkbook. He opened his checkbook and said, "I hope that this covers most of your bills." He wrote a check for two hundred thousand dollars. "See Kerry. Pay it forward ten fold." Carl said to Kerry. "Thank you so much and God bless you. Do you want to stay for dinner Dr. Curtis?"

Carl asked with Kerry in agreement. "I better be going soon. I got to get back home to my wife. Thanks for the offer and maybe some other time if the offer still stands, my wife and I will come over." Dr. Curtis said. "Yes, of course." Said Kerry. "Thank you so much for all you have done. It has been such a blessing. It has also been an honor knowing you and being able to help you. Do you have any idea as to how great your treasures are? I mean, people that don't know God, also known as atheists, build up and store up earthly treasures that they can't take with them when they are gone. People who know Christ, also known as Christians, build up and store up treasures in heaven. The treasures in heaven are so much more great and better than those here on earth. In the Bible it talks about building up treasures in heaven and going to the place that I have prepared for you.

Wow how much more inspirational can you get? I mean, God's treasures are mansions and streets of gold and enter that through pearly white gates. The biggest treasure that God has for us though is to be able to enter the pearly white gates of heaven. To live there with God for eternity and just knowing, believing and having faith is the greatest gift. Wow, how amazing is that?" Carl said through tears of joy and happiness. "Your welcome and maybe sometime my wife, Linda and I can start coming over for Bible studies. That would greatly not only help me out but, also help Linda get to come to know Christ as the Lord and personal Savior. That would make me happy. To know that she would be with us in heaven." Dr. Curtis stated. "Yes, it would and we would be honored to do that for you and for Linda." Kerry said.

"You are more than gracious. God will reward you handsomely." Dr. Curtis said. "We don't really care about getting rewarded. That is not why we do what we do. We do it because that is God's calling on our life and in our hearts." Carl stated. "Yes, I know. Well I better get back home. Glad your ok and I'm also glad you got to come home." Dr. Curtis said. "Thanks again for everything. If you need anything and I mean anything, call us. We would be more then happy and glad to help." Carl said. They all walked out to the front yard where Carl could sit down on a lawn chair. They said good-bye to Dr. Curtis and he left. "Do you think that driver needs another drink?" Kerry asked. "You could ask him." Carl said. With that being said Kerry and Carl walked slowly into the house.

Carl sat on the couch while Kerry went to ask the driver if he needed something else to drink. Carl saw Kerry pass a couple of times. When she went to go pass by again, Carl stopped her and asked, "Kerry, what are you doing?" I'm trying to find the driver. His truck isn't outside and he is no where to be found. Your bed is all set up so maybe he left. Do you think?" Kerry asked. "Well maybe. Then again maybe he didn't want to be rude and interrupt our conversation." Carl said. "Maybe your right." Kerry stated and walked to the kitchen to make lunch. The phone range and Carl picked up. "Benton residence, Carl speaking how can I help you?" Call said as he answered the phone. "Yes Mr. Benton this is Bill how are you doing?" Bill stated, in amazement that Carl answered since he was supposed to be resting. "Good. Wore out and tired, but handling it with God's and Kerry's help."

"Well that's good. I was just calling to ask if I can bring the kids by to see you, or if it would be too much on you?" Bill asked. "Yeah, yeah, that would be great. Hey how about you guys come over for dinner tonight? We can see the kids and all catch up then." Carl said. "Yes, that would be great. What time?" "Hold on let me get Kerry. Kerry Bill is on the phone and wants to speak with you." Carl hollered to her still sitting on the couch. Kerry walked into the room and got the phone from Carl and answered it. "Hello brother how are you doing?" Kerry asked. "Good, just wanted to know what time you wanted us there for dinner tonight? Carl invited us over. I hope that is ok." Bill stated. "Oh yes, that's good. Um, let me think here. How about six O' clock. That will give me time to get everything ready." Kerry replied. "Ok, see you then Kerry. I love you." "I love you to See you then." Kerry sated back.

Six-fifteen p.m. Bill, Kim, Jacob and Hailley walked into the house. "Hi mom, where's dad?" Little Jacob asked. "He's in the family room on the couch, but please be careful with him dear." Kerry told Jacob. "Yes mom, thanks." Jacob told his mom. Jacob and Hailley started going towards the family room, stopped, turned around, walked back to Kerry and gave her a hug and told her they loved her and then they both ran off." "Hi Kerry. How's he doing?" Kim asked. "Good. He gets tired easy, but that is easy to do when he won't sit still. Plus he gets winded pretty easy." Kerry stated. "Well, that will all pass with time. Healing takes a while but he will heal." Kim said. "Yes. I know. God has healed his body faster than anyone has ever seen before. Thank God he's home, but still praying God continues his work in him." Kerry said.

"He will my dear. God will never take, or lift his hand from Carl. Carl is a very strong man of God and his faith is amazing. Carl truly is a man of God." Bill said. "Yes, I know." Kerry replied. They all walked into the family room and started talking when Kerry states, "Well Bill. You got here late as usual, but you got here and safe." "Yeah, well. If I'm not late then that would just break my routine of things." Bill said. "Hey, maybe if we would have stated to come over at five forty-five p.m. then you would have been here at six p.m. sharp." Carl said with a chuckle and then everyone started laughing. "We will be leaving tomorrow for that tournament. I just wanted you guys to see the kids before we left." Bill stated. "Thanks. It is good to see them, but I do still need to rest.

By the time you get back then I should have been rested up." Carl said. "Ok, sounds good." Bill replied. "Now that that is all settled. I have a question. Where will Hailley be during the week that you are gone?" Kerry asked. "She will be at home with me." Kim stated. "Ok, sounds good." Kerry said. After dinner, which was mashed potatoes, green bean casserole and a large pot roast with sparkling cider for the drinks, they said good-bye and left to get packed and ready for bed. "Do you want to take a hot bath or just go to bed and take one in the morning?" Kerry asked Carl. "I'll take one in the morning. I'm tuckered tonight. It has been a very, very long day." Carl told Kerry. "Ok, then would you like me to help you get ready for bed?" Kerry asked Carl. "With all my heart. Thanks love." Carl said.

After Kerry got Carl ready for bed and tucked in, she sat on the side of the bed and read Ecc. three to Carl. "That is my favorite chapter in that book because it is so true. There is a time for everything under the heavens. The only thing is, is it is all in God's timing that things happen and not our timing. Thank you so much for that scripture. I really needed that and it was perfect." Carl said to Kerry. "Hey now. Don't you be thanking me. I just read what God told someone else to write. So the person to actually be thanking is God. Speaking of thanking God, let us pray." Kerry said. After they got done praying it was ten O'clock p.m. Kerry said good-night, told Carl she loved him and kissed him ever so gently and then went to bed. Carl woke up several times through out the night. Kerry came and checked on Carl several times during the night.

The next morning at seven O'clock a.m. Kerry came downstairs and made a pot of coffee. She heard something wrustle in the bedroom so she went to see if Carl was up yet. She peaked in and saw that Carl was still fast asleep, laying on his left side, facing the door, with his right arm stretched over top his head and pillow. His left leg was straight and his right leg was bent up to his stomach. She saw that he was comfortable so she slipped back into the kitchen to make breakfast. She made eggs Benedict, waffles, sausage and a hot pot of coffee. When she was done making a plate for Carl, she put his plate, coffee, fork, spoon and napkin on the serving tray and took it to him. "Honey. Time to get up. Breakfast time."

After putting Carl's bed in a sitting position. Carl sat up and she eased the tray onto Carl's lap. "Is that ok dear?" Kerry asked, not wanting the pain to get worse. "Yes dear. It is. Can you please get me a pain pill?" Carl asked. Now Carl is a hot shot. He doesn't like to show that he is in pain, but it was unbearable in the mornings. "Yes dear. I will get you the other meds also. The nurse will be here at ten a.m." Kerry told Carl. "Ok, I'm going to need a shower this morning." Carl stated. "I kinda though so. I put all clean towels and wash clothes in there. The floor mat and rugs are all washed ad I hung your clothes up in there for you to get dressed." Kerry said. "Well thank you. Please don't tell me I have to wear jeans. You know I don't like them." Carl retorted.

"No. I places some of your comfy sweats you really like and a t-shirt in there." Kerry said with a large grin. "Awesome, much appreciated. Hey if you want to, you can join me in the shower." Carl stated and then winked as if hinting at something more then just a shower. "Well, I would love, but, I already took one this morning and I'm sure that you need your personal time also. You need to heal up a little before any of that goes on my dear. Thanks for the gesture though. It made me feel good, wanted and needed." Kerry replied. "Honey. You should always feel that way." Carl said. "I know but lately I feel helpless because I wasn't able to help you. You had doctors and nurses doing everything for you and I felt like a bystander." Kerry said. "Kerry. You have been doing more for me than any doctor or nurse or anybody, but, God every could." Carl said taking her hand in his.

"Yeah and how's that?" Kerry asked. "If it wasn't for your prayers and God listening and answering. I honestly don't believe that I would be home, at this house, with you today. I honestly think that I would be walking side by side with God." Carl said. Kerry looked into his eyes, blinked and a tear rolled down her cheek. "Please don't cry darling. I am just telling you the truth. I honestly don't mean to make you cry." Carl said softly with the words to try and comfort. "No dear. These are tears of joy. I'm just so happy that you feel that way. I love you." Kerry took the left side of his head with her right hand and her thumb gently caressing his cheek and bent over and kissed him. After Carl showered and shaved, he walked into the living room where Kerry was sitting. "Oooo. Hey good looking. How do you feel?" Kerry asked.

"Good. Much better, and the water was actually hot and stayed hot. That is more then I can say for the hospital showers. Hey I'm thankful and very grateful that I even got a shower there." Carl said and sat down on the big comfy couch next to Kerry. After the nurse came and checked Carl out, drew his blood and did vitals, she told us she would have Dr. Curtis give us a call with the results. "Ok, thank you very much and God bless." Kerry and Carl responded. With that the nurse walked out and was gone.

Chapter 5

CONFRONTING THE PERPETRATOR

Later that evening, the phone rang. Kerry's heart felt like it was in her throat. She thought that it was another bad call, knowing that Bill and Jacob flew to Idaho for that tournament. She was thinking that it was going to be the call telling her that the plane crashed and everyone was either killed or not found yet, but not survivors. With her luck that might as well be the case. "No, Kerry. You have got to stop thinking those awful thought. Devil, I rebuke you in the name of Jesus and command you to leave." Kerry told herself and then answered the phone. "Hello." Kerry said kind of softly when she did pick up. "Yes. Is this the Benton Residence?" Answered the caller. "Yes it is. May I ask who's calling?" Kerry stated. "Yes, this is the New York police department and my name is Alice. Sheriff Fang wanted me to call and make arrangements to come speak with you. It is very urgent. How does tomorrow morning sound for you?" Replied the officer. "Ok, good. May I ask what this is regarding?" Kerry asked.

"Mam, at this time I'm not able to give out too much information, but it has to do with the shoot out at the Central Station. I believe your husband was involved. It has to do with other information that came up and he has some questions to ask?' Replied Alice. "Ok, I'll let him know and eleven a.m. sounds good. We shall speak to him then. Thanks for calling." Kerry stated and hung up the phone. Kerry walked into Carl's bedroom and told Carl what Officer Alice had told her on the phone and that Sheriff Fang would be here tomorrow at eleven a.m. to talk. "He is pretty punctual. That means that he will either be here at eleven or a little earlier." Carl stated. "Ok, no worries. We will have everything done and waiting on him then." Kerry said. With that being said, they said good-night. Kerry was so tired that by ten thirty a.m., she had just gotten up and dressed. ten forty-five, there was a knock on the door. Carl answered it. "Hi, boss. How is work going?" Carl said when he opened the door and saw that it was his boss.

"As good as it gets. How are you doing? You look great. I thought that you would have looked a lot worse after what was told to me and the pictures that I saw of the scene." Sheriff Fang stated. "No. It really wasn't that bad. Well not as bad as what pictures show. It could have been a lot worse. Thank God it wasn't though. Thank God for a speedy recovery also." Carl stated as he ushered Mr. Fang to the living room. Kerry walked in at this time with a flowered dress on and a shawl around her shoulders. "May I interest you in something to drink or eat?" Kerry said looking at Fang as if she knew he was going to say something good. "Yes, I will have a cup of coffee with a spoonful of honey please." Sheriff Fang answered. "For you dear?" "I'll have a cup of coffee to please." replied Carl. While Kerry was in the kitchen getting the drinks, Carl told his boss to hold up on talk about the case until Kerry came back. "I'll respect the." Fang replied. Mean while in the kitchen Kerry made a fresh pot of coffee and had warmed up some of her famous sugar cookies.

Putting them on a platter ready to be served she walked back into the living room and put the platter with the cookies and coffee on the table. She handed everyone their coffee and then sat next to Carl on the couch. "Oh, Mrs. Benton, these cookies are delicious, and the coffee is excellent also. Thank you so very much. I needed a good cup of coffee today. The coffee at the station always seems to taste so stale." Said Sheriff Fang. "Well thank you. Any time you want a cup and your on duty then just call and I'll have one ready for you when you arrive." Kerry replied. "Will do. Thanks. Now then, onto business. I have in good authority who the perpetrators are in this whole Central Station ordeal. I know for a fact that there were two girls and two boys involved. It all started when the kids robbed a liquor store and then took it to Central Station after not getting caught. The teens all got drunk and fired a couple shots, just playing around.

In the midst of doing that both girls got shot and killed. By the time police arrived, the girls were already dead and the boys were so scared that they freaked out and started shooting i.e. police officers were hurt and killed. We have the names of the boys involved and would like to confront them in court. The date is set for this coming Tuesday at ten a.m. If you would like to give your statement then please be there. If not then you will really have no say as to what happens to the boys. So if I may say, I really hope you do show up and give your statement as it will also better help the judge understand the motive of what all took place and to hear all sides of the story." Sheriff Fang said with little emotion until he was practically telling, not asking them to show up and give statements. "We will most assuredly be there and with statements t give. Do we need to write what happened now and give them to you?" Carl asked.

"I see that you did read the fine print of the handbook. The section where it states that if your are not working and police are called, you are to act as if you are not employed with the department. Good for you. Yes that is the deal. I will look over them and then submit them to the court once I get them all." Sheriff Fang stated. "Ok, if you would like to come back at two p.m. we will have them ready for pick up." Carl stated. "I have a meeting at that time, but if you don't mind dropping them off at the station, I would appreciate it." Fang replied. "Sure thing. Oh and by the way, it has been really good seeing you again." Carl stated. "Yeah, you to. When are you coming back to work?" "They told me ten weeks and it has only been two weeks but, we will see. I don't know quite yet to be exact." Carl said. "Ok, we will see you soon then. Thanks again for the coffee and cookies." "Your more then welcome. Anytime." Was all Kerry could find herself to say because she knew exactly what she wanted to say to the boys but, is going to have to pray about it.

By one O'clock p.m. both Kerry and Carl were done writing out their statements. Exactly like Carl said at two O'clock p.m. they had gone to the police station and turned in their statements to the clerk there. Carl and Kerry both took day to day activities very hard until the trial day. It seemed to Kerry that even the easiest task, like cooking dinner for them both, seemed to be as hard as the first time driving a car. Meaning that having to remember everything, part of it. For Carl, it was more or less that he just didn't want to do anything. So finally the day of the trial comes and Carl and Kerry want to make sure that they get there on time. They arrived at nine a.m. Having to sit and wait in anticipation was better then being at home and in fear of being late or something. The closer that time was nearing until the trial started was agonizing. Carl and Kerry both kept seeing teenagers come in and walk out. They wondered if by chance one of them just might have been the one to shoot Carl.

By happen stance, they were both wrong. None of the teens that came in was the one. By ten minutes 'till trial started, Kerry was so nervous to actually see the face of the person who shot her husband, and what she might do or say at that time. She had to excuse herself and use the restroom to take a short breather, and to pray. By the time that Kerry returned to her seat the courtroom was packed. Not only with officers on and off duty, but by whiteness's and family members of the people injured or killed. They were all ready and willing to stand up and give their testimony, and say what they think just punishment the boys should have. She quietly took her seat. Slipping by Carl who was seated on the end, and maneuvering to get comfortable on the hard bench seats in the audience. Just waiting to see what happens, and to be called. "have you seen him yet?" Kerry leaned over and whispered in Carl's ear. "Not yet. They haven't brought him out yet." Carl responded. When the judge came in, like always, they had to stand and then sit.

All waiting as patient as can be until it was their turn to tell their side of the story. The first to be called, was the wife of one officer that was killed. Her story touched everyone.

Kerry found herself crying. "We should have brought some tissues with us." Kerry said to Carl. Carl was trying to pay attention to what was being said on the stand, and then Kerry's words "We should have brought tissues with us." kept coming back to his mind. So Carl reached into the side pocket of his sports jacket and took out his un-used "snot rag" and gave it to Kerry, still enthralled by what was being said on the stand by each person. After going through ten people, the judge called for an hour recess. This was good considering the fact that it was lunch time and Carl had to use the restroom really bad, but didn't in fear of missing something important. When Carl returned from the restroom, Kerry asked him, "What would you like for lunch?" Carl looked at her and responded, "Lunch! How can you be thinking about lunch at a time like this? Besides, I thought you were nervous?"

"Well, actually, I was. I also prayed about it and God touched me, softened my heart and calmed my spirit." Kerry replied. "Ok, then lets get something small. We don't want to be late getting back to the courtroom. What about a hamburger?" Carl asked rhetorically. "Sounds good." Walking across the street to Jeff's Burger Palace, Kerry asked another question. "Carl, now that we are here, what kind of burger do you want?" "A regular burger." Carl stated. After ordering they sat down at an outside table to the restaurant and prayed before eating. A guy that looked, and smelt like he had not taken a bath in years came up. "Your faith in God is great and your treasures in heaven are far more than you realize." The old, raggedy looking man stated and then was gone. Suddenly a man in a business suite came up and stood right behind Kerry. Carl looked up and said, "I have seen you before, oh wait, you are one of the lawyers doing the questioning in our courtroom." "Depends. What courtroom are we talking about here?" Look at him with eyes ablaze. "102 and it is the Central Station case."

Carl was now sitting straight up and his arms were resting on the table, as if putting up a front, just in case something did happen. "Yes sir, I am. I can tell you sir that you are next." With that being said he walked off. Kerry turned around to see who Carl was talking to, but didn't see anyone. "Carl, honey. You need to eat so we can get back to the courtroom." Kerry said in a rushed, calm like manor. Carl scarffed the last four bites of his burger. He threw his and Kerry's garbage in the trash while Kerry was gathering everything else. Upon entering the courtroom, it was all packed again and there was only two seats left. They were against the back wall. Carl took one of the seats and then pointed to the chair next to him for Kerry to sit down. When the judge entered, they found themselves having to stand back up and then sit right back down. "Who is your next whiteness in this case?" The judge asked. "I would now like to call Carl Benton to the stand." The lawyer in the grey suite said upon standing. Carl's eyes opened wide as he stood up and started walking to the stand. After getting sworn in and seated, the judge told the lawyer to proceed.

"Is it or is it not true Mr. Benton, that you work for the sheriffs office for Central Division?" The lawyer asked. Yes sir. It is true." Carl responded. "What unit are you from then?" "I'm counted as the first class unit twelve for my division, but sir. I don't see how what unit I'm from is relevant to any of what happened because all units were called to the scene that night." Carl replied. "Oh, so you don't see how your unit is relevant? Let me tell you. You just stated to the court that you were from unit twelve "first class", and that would be k-9 correct?" The lawyer glared at Carl. "Yes sir. That is correct. Now if you would just let me get on with telling my testimony as to what really happened that night. I'm sure that you will get all of the answers that you need to all of your questions." Carl stated back kind of firm. "Ok, please do tell the court what really happened that night." The lawyer stated rhetorically. Carl told his side of the story. It took forever and a day it seemed like, but, he got into very detailed description. All the way down to the pain he felt when he got shot. After finishing the story the lawyer asked.

"How did you get shot in your abdomen, if you were wearing your bullet proof vest, Mr. Benton?" "Well, sir. As all policemen know that a bullet proof vest does not stop bullets from coming from the side. At the time that I was shot there, I was already turned to the side looking at my partner who was shot and laying on the ground next to me. I have already stated this in my testimony that I had just recently told the court." Carl replied. "So you were turned to the side then?" "Yes sir. I was. I can't tell you much after that because I blacked out from loss of blood. Thanks be to God who does merecals, I wouldn't be here today." Carl said. "Ok. So in your own words verbally, because I already know that you have a written statement submitted with the courts, but in words, please tell the court what you feel an acceptable just punishment would be for this vial act." The lawyer stated.

"First of all I would have to say that I honestly don't believe that..." Carl stopped and looked at the judge and asked, "I believe sir, that it would be most beneficial to the court and to you for better judgment, if I was able to speak openly, and without interruptions from the prosecutor." Carl said. "So be it." The judge stated and then banged his gavel in agreement. "I honestly believe that the kids didn't meant to do the shooting. I mean, if only one of you has ever gotten so scared when you were younger, or even now, that you did something wrong, then you should have gotten jail time or worse for your crime also. Seeing that the robbing was a big deal that they were under aged. Then yes, community service is a good thing. As far as the shooting goes. They were all under aged intoxicated, scared kids who got really freaked out, and should not get jailed but to spend one year in a good church, front row. I am not making any excuses for these children and I am not saying that all of these kind of crimes should be let loose like this, but, I am saying that instead of going straight to something, take a step back and look at what you did when you were a child and see if it called for jail time and then come back to reality and make your judgment then. I know how adults can get when they get drunk. Can you just imagine what the kids were thinking though? I know that I can't. If it pleases the courts I would be honored to have these children attend my church, front row, accompanied by myself and my wife and their Bibles. You would and will be surprised at what a change can be made and God will prove that to all of you. Thank you. Carl stated.

Carl looked back at Kerry who by now was bawling silently, and she gave him a thumbs up. "So what your telling me is, that instead of giving the children punishment, you want to make it to where they can still roam free, do what they want, when they want to do it, but, go and attend your church every Sunday for one full year and one full year of community service?" Lawyer asked. "Yes dir. I am. Like I stated just a second ago, the children were belligerently drunk. I know that you have been drunk, and probably did some vial things yourself, but, your not found under aged. You think that God loves them any less because they were under aged and drunk? Well then God would love you less because you get crazy also when you get drunk. NO! God loves us all the same and wants to see everyone succeed and this is just the start for these children. If you want to put them in jail then fine, but let me tell you this one thing. If you do put them in jail then it will scare them so bad that they will be scared to do anything, and I mean that and that would include lifting a fork to eat their dinner, in fear that they will go back to jail. I think that seeing the girls die was enough punishment for a youngster to see because now they have to live with that regret the rest of their lives.

God is a just, forgiving and loving God. He has and will forgive them boys. When they ask of it from Him." Carl replied. "No further questions your honor." The lawyer stated. "Do you wish to cross examine the whiteness?" The judged asked. "NO sir. The whiteness made his statement very clear and detailed." The judge then stated, "Thank you sir and now you may step down." Carl nodded in agreement. Carl then went back to his seat. After writing some things down the judge then asked if there was any other whiteness's that he would like to question. "Yes sir. There is one last whiteness. If she would like to testify, that is Mrs. Benton." The lawyer stated. Kerry looked at Carl and then stood. Before she moved from her seat she stated. "I will testify only if I openly and without interruptions as did my husband Carl Benton." "Proceed." The judge stated and then once again smacked his gavel to confirm. Once Kerry was sworn in and seated her first question came. "Do you love your husband?" The lawyer asked.

"Yes sir. I do. Like Carl said, what does love have to do with this vial act that has been already forgiven? It has been forgiven from my husband, who was critically injured. Forgiven by his family, who had to go through all of the suffering and still have to live everyday knowing that that could have been his very last. Ultimately and foremost, forgive by the one who gave him his very existence of life, and that is God. That is the most important forgiveness of all." Kerry replied. "Good, then you don't mind answering this. If Carl as you say, was so critically injured or hurt, then why is he here today and not still in the hospital?" Asked the prosecutor. "That is a very easy question to answer. If you have any faith at all and believe with all your heart and trust God with all your mind, body, soul and strength, then you know that is God wanted to heal him he would have. Whether it would have been to take Carl home to be with him or to heal him physically. God chose to give Carl physical healing because it is not yet Carl's time and only God can give and take life.

Not man. God is the one true judge that really matters. God has already made judgment on those poor boys and has dealt with accordingly. To punish them further, that is a crime in itself." Kerry replied. "No further questions your honor." The prosecutor stated. "Would you like to cross examine?" Asked the judge. "No sir, her statement was satisfactory." "Thank you, you may step down." The judge stated. When Kerry got back to her seat Carl kissed her and told her good job. "I wanted to say more but it is getting late." Kerry replied. "Is there any more whiteness's that have not been called yet or, is there anyone else that has not testified that would like to before the defendant enters and no more will be said and the courtroom will stay quiet and behind the floor?" The judge asked. No one stood up. No one rose a hand. No one said a word. Rather everyone gripped their chairs and benches and locked their jaws as you can see everyone's face tighten.

"Please officer, if you would bring the first boy in." The judge asked. The officer opened the door next to the judges seat and disappeared for about two minutes. When the door finally opened again a young male, with bright red, spiked hair, orange outfit and chains with handcuffs around his wrists to his waist and down to his ankles followed by two police officers that doubled his size. After getting sworn in and shackled to his chair, the first question came. "Will you please state your name for the court?" The lawyer asked. "My name is Alex Defoy." Said the young man. "Thank you. Now if you would, because everyone is really wanting to know why you did it. Please explain your side to the court for better understanding." The lawyer said. "Yes sir." As he told his side, he started to cry and fold under pressure. Once he stopped, the prosecutor asked him if there was anything else that he would like to add before he leaves and is dismissed. The boy solemnly said, "I just want to tell everyone's family who got killed, how gratefully sorry I am and I live with the picture of that day over and over replaying in my mind, as if it just happened.

For the peoples families that are here and got injured. I want to say that I am gratefully sorry for disfiguring you and I want you to know that my heart aches and my heart itself is disfigured. My heart is inside, so you are not able to see it, but, it is the truth and you, you are not able to hide your disfigurement like I can. I honestly don't know what else I am able to say to make things better, but, I can say this. Whatever punishment I get. I truly deserve, as my actions were a disgrace, undeserving, disgusting and dishonorable to anyone who's anyone. I am sorry and deserve what is coming to me." The boy stated through sobs, tears and a hanging head. "No further questions your honor." The lawyer said. The judge simply looked at the boy who truely looked sad and sincerely sorry and told him that he was dismissed. The boy stepped down and went back through the door followed by the officers that clearly towered over him. The next boy refused to testify. That was clear, he was the one who started it.

The courtroom fell deathly silent as the judge was writing stuff down. When the judge looked up, he called for this to be recessed until tomorrow morning at eight a.m. to give the jury time to think and give their opinions. On the ride home Kerry couldn't help but state how she felt. "Did you see that boy? He truly looked sincere when he was talking. He was crying. If he was not sorry for what he did, he would not have cried and said what he did. He would have been like the other boy who didn't testify." Kerry Stated. "Tomorrow is the moment of truth. All we can do now is pray that God soften hearts." The rest of that night and until the got back to the courtroom, Kerry and Carl hardly conversed. "Today seems like the room is more packed to me. Does it to you Carl?" Kerry asked. No answer. Carl was in a study state of prayer. The bailiff said, "All rise, the court is now in session etc..." "You may be seated." The judge stated. "Has the jury come to a conclusion as of yesterdays testimonies?" The judge asked.

An older man stood up. He was tall, going bald. looked like a helicopter pad on his head, wearing white slacks and a blue and grey stripped shirt. He began. "In the case of Alex Defoy, We the jury find the defendant..." There was a long pause. It seemed as though they needed more time because it sounded like the guy was still unsure as to his answer. "Guilty at the account of vial disgrace and undignified actions." The man stated. He sat down as he was done stating the results. "I hereby declare that Alex Defoy and Kenneth Williams guilty to the hereby allegations and sentenced to one full year of church services, every Sunday morning accompanied by Carl and Kerry Benton, who will call Mondays to let the court know if they showed or not. Also they both have one full year of community service as directed..." The judge stated and then slammed his gavel on the wooden pallet to seal the deal. After the court was over, Carl went up to Alex and Kenneth and gave them both hugs and looked each one in the eyes and said, "I forgive you and so does my wife and our family. See you Sunday at East Coast Community Church at eight a.m. sharp." Carl said. He hugged both boys again and then walked away.

Chapter 6

CONVERTING

It was a pretty good day in May. The sun was shinning, the wind was slightly blowing and it was the very first Sunday of May, the very first Sunday of the boys coming to church. Seven forty-five a.m. and everyone was starting to pile into the church. Carl and Kerry stood outside to greet people as they came in. They didn't see Kenneth or Alex yet, but, that is not to say that they won't show because they told them eight O'clock a.m. A car pulled up that they have never seen in church before. Yet it wasn't new, didn't have fancy thing on it or anything like that. The engine cut off but no one got out yet. Seven fifty-five and finally the door ajared. Firth thing they saw was red spiked hair. Carl just knew that it was Alex, so he got a large grin across his face. Alex came walking up to Carl and Kerry and said hello. He was wearing pretty nice blue jeans, a white polo shirt and Nike Air tennishoes. "You look good and I'm glad to see you." Carl said. Kerry couldn't find any words to say at all so she just smiled.

"We have to wait for Kenneth now and then we can go in." Carl stated. Sure enough a large, white escalade pulled into the parking lot and Kenneth got out. He was wearing tan khakis with a blue and white with grey stripped nice dress shirt and dress shoes. "Now. I'm not doing this because I want to or because I like dressing this way, but, my mom made me dress this way and told me I was very lucky that this was the only punishment that I received. She also told me that if it was her, then she would have done a lot worse, but, you had compassion and forgiveness, and even though you were the one I hurt." Kenneth stated and then followed that with, "Lets just go in and get this over with so I can go home and sleep." "It is nice to see you here and you look good." Carl responded to all that. Alex just glared at Kenneth. As praise and worship was going on the boys stayed seated, while everyone else stood. After praise and worship was over with it was time for sharing, praise reports, prayer requests, etc...

During this time, Carl stood up and introduced Alex and Kenneth as his friends. Alex rose to his feet to be acknowledged, but Kenneth still sat but raised his hand. Pastor Gregg asked the boys if they had anything that they would like to share. Alex stood up again and said, "I'm thankful for a very just punishment." "This is the one who shot my leg and my face, Kenneth is the one who took the other shots at me. I will give testimony to that also, later on." Carl declared and both Carl and Alex sat down. Kerry took the spare Bibles that were under the pews for people who forgot theirs and handed one to Kenneth and one to Alex. Alex said thanks and set it in his lap, but Kenneth didn't say anything and put his next to him. Pastor Greg then asked Carl if he would like to come up and preach/testimony today. "Yes I would." Carl replied. Right before church ended at twelve twenty-five p.m. Carl made sure to point out loud and clear that next service is at eight O'clock a.m. sharp next Sunday and to make sure and join us. After service Kenneth rushed out. "I don't think that he could have left any faster." Kerry remarked.

Alex stayed a while to talk with Carl and Kerry while waiting for his ride to come. When his ride showed up he left. Carl and Kerry went on home and prayed about the events that took place that morning and then ate dinner and went to bed. Early the next morning Kerry got up. She had noticed that things were moved around in the house. She walked into the family room where most of the pictures of the kids and family was, she noticed that some were off the walls and laying broken and shattered on the ground. She quickly walked to the front door and saw that it was still locked. She then looked at the security system to find it still turned on. Kerry then went to the kitchen to check the garage door. It was locked also. Kerry made her rounds around the house and found that every door and window was still shut and locked. "What on earth could have happened then to make everything move and pictures fall and break like that?" She asked herself walking to Carl's room. When she entered his room she saw that he was still asleep. She shook his left shoulder gently, and said, she loved him, good morning and that everything was moved.

"What do you mean everything is moved? Did you redecorate and I slept through it?" Carl was not yet finished talking when Kerry interrupted him saying, "The pictures of the kids when they were babies and the family portrait is also laying on the floor and the glass shattered out. I checked all the doors and windows and they are all still locked and the security system is still activated." Kerry said, kind of in a monetary, rushed, scared tone. Carl quickly sat up on the edge of the bed and took Kerry in his arms. "Did the pictures get damaged or was it just the glass and the frames that broke?" Carl asked Kerry. All Carl could hear was sobbing until she said, "The pictures are fine but still, I don't know what happened. It is gloomy outside but there is no damage to the yard or any other parts of the house." "Lets go take the pictures and put them up. We will then watch the news to see what happened if anything." Carl told Kerry. Carl started to get a little paranoid also

43

but still had to be strong for Kerry's sake. On the news, channel nine WNBC, there was a report that a massive earthquake hit downtown New York.

Carl turned to Kerry, more relieved to have heard that it was just an earthquake instead of something more serious. He tried to comfort Kerry by saying, "See honey it was just a earthquake. Nothing more, nothing less. Does that ease your mind a little more? I just can't believe that we slept through it!" Carl stated and then pulled Kerry a little closer to him and kissed her on the forehead. "Yes it does dear. You know, why is every bad thing happening now? I mean all at once. I just don't understand. Well maybe there is a good reason but we just need to wait and see what that reason is. I'm going to have to pray and ask God to ease my feelings because right now I'm feeling mixed." Kerry replied. "You do that. While your doing that I will clean up a little bit." Carl stated and then followed it with, "and after I'm done and dressed and have had breakfast, how about we go and get some more picture frames? How does that sound?" Carl asked Kerry. She didn't respond but she did nod her head and kissed him. When Carl and Kerry got back from town they put the new frames on the table and put the pictures inside after first cleaning all the glass. Picture by picture was getting placed back in it's original place. Kerry felt more at ease. After placing the last picture n the wall, Kerry told Carl that she was going to take a long hot bath. "Are you going to be ok darling?" Kerry asked Carl. "Yes dear. I think I'll just sit here on the couch and watch some T.V. or read the mornings paper." Carl replied. With that Kerry gave him a long well deserved kiss that was long overdue. While Kerry was in the bath, about twenty minutes in, he heard a knock on their door. When he opened the door, he saw that it was his neighbor, Mr. Kline. "Hello, may I help you?" Carl asked. "Not necessarily help me but tell me a few things." Mr. Kline retorted. "Ok, well um, come on in. Have a seat and we'll talk." "Thank you very much." Said Mr. Kline. A few moments passed and Carl asked, "So what can I help you with Mr. Kline?" Carl asked, still pondering the thought of why he would come to him because he never did before. Just said hello over the fence. "My first question is, and you can take this how you want to, but, are you happy in your marriage Mr. Benton?"

Mr. Kline asked with a little distortment look on his face, with his head cocked to the left a little. "Woe there Mr. Kline. Don't you think that is a little too personal of a question to be asking?" Carl responded. Kind of offended by this question. "Yes sir. It is a personal question but it is a very clear question and there is a reason I'm asking Mr. Benton. So if you would be so kind as to answer my question, I would be obliged." Retorted Mr. Kline. "Ok, well let me see how to put this. Yes I am very, very happy with my wife. I love you like I have never loved another girl. Well to me she is no girl, she is a woman. She is everything that I wanted and more. She also in turn makes me very happy, and that is a good thing. See when I was with my ex, I didn't really know what love was. Then God showed me what love was and how to love someone. Then God showed me in the Bible where it states, not to be un-equally yoked. I did all that was asked. She left me because I had changed. She didn't like the new me. I didn't care though. When I met Kerry, she told me what she was all about. That she was God driven and I respected that. That was the main thing I wanted in a woman and she had it.

She had much more than I was looking for also, but, that is not why I married her. She is a Godly woman. That is why I married her. She let me love her for her and because I showed her God's love for her from God's love within me, we fit perfectly. So to answer your question as to if I'm happy in my marriage? The answer is yes. Without a doubt." Carl replied. "That's good. Now my second question would be..." There was a long pause. Almost as if he was trying to think of a question on the sport. "I was watching the news and saw what happened at Central Station. So what al did happen?" Mr. Kline asked. In the middle of Carl explaining what had happened, up until the boys coming to church order, Kerry walked in. "Oh. Mr. Kline. How are you?" Kerry said in an undoubtedly shocked tone with a little worry to top it all off. "I'm good Mrs. Benton. Thanks for asking. I just came by to check on Carl ad to see what happened at Central Station." Mr. Kline replied, moving his hand closer to his private areas where an erecting had already formed. "Mr. Kline was just leaving." Carl said as he saw this action taking place.

"Well, thanks for the talk and I bid you good day folks." Mr. Kline stated as he was ushered to and out the door. Upon closing the door, Kerry took Carl into the bedroom where Carl slept for the past couple weeks. "Have a seat. Your going to need it." "What is it Kerry? Why is it that right when you come into the room, did Mr. Kline, decide to want to touch himself. I mean right in front of me, and being so disrespectful in our house?" Carl couldn't believe it. "The day that got the call I was getting the kids in the car. I had just buckled Jacob in his seat, when I noticed Mr. Kline standing on his porch. He was watching and then he said hello." Kerry shuttered. "So what is wrong with Mr. Kline saying hello?" Carl stated. "Well, he didn't just say hello. He started moving closer and closer to the gate and just kept wanting to talk. I was thinking about you and it was Really starting to really freak me out. Honey, not only that but he has been watching me for a while now and I really don't like it." Kerry said hugging herself in discussed. "Well, my dear. Why didn't you tell me this sooner? I would not have allowed him into our house.

It is my duty to protect you and the children. If you don't tell me things, then how am I to do anything about it?" Carl asked. "With everything that was going on. I knew that you had enough to be concerned about that you didn't need to be concerned with this also. I was going to tell you later and not tell you right off the bat, so you could rest and not get too riled up again about something. It would have taken some time but I would have eventually told you. Don't think that I would not have because I would have believe me. That guy gives me the heebie-jeebies." Kerry told Carl. "Ok dear. I believe you. I will deal with this issue soon. Do me a favor and the next time that you have something that is even the slightest bit unnerving to you, please tell me right away and don't wait ok? Promise me dear?" Carl asked while looking Kerry dead in the eyes so she knew that he was dead serious. "Yes dear. I promise." Kerry said returning the look. Kerry placed her right hand on Carl's left cheek, and Carl placed his left hand on Kerry's right cheek, they leaned into a warm, wet, long lasting kiss that was interrupted by the phone ringing.

"I'll get it." Carl said. Carl walked over into the family room and picked up the phone. "Benton residence, Carl speaking." "Mr. Benton." The voice replied shakily. "Yes. May I ask who's calling?" "Will you please come get me? I'm scared and I will explain everything later to you." The voice replied in a sobering manor. "Where are you?" Asked Carl. "I'm at 5th and Crosby Ave. At the Chevron station. Please hurry before he comes to get me." The phone went silent and he knew right then and there that he had to go. "Kerry, I got an estranged call and he asked me to come and get him. He said that he was scared and didn't want him to come back. Will you drive? He's at 5th and Crosby, at the Chevron Station. He sounded like he was crying." Carl told Kerry upon entering the room. After getting dressed they got into the and started on their way. All the while on the drive Carl was praying out loud and Kerry was nodding in agreement and said "Yes Lord." When they got to the gas station, Carl went into the store and asked the station attendant if she had seen someone use the phone. "Yes sir and then he walked out and to the right of the building. She replied.

"Thank you." Carl sparked. Carl gently nodded his head to her and walked through the doubled doors. As he walked out he turned to the right and walked to the end of the building. He didn't see anyone. So he said in a pretty loud, pretty clear voice, "Hello. This is Carl Benton. Did someone call me from the phone here?" He stated. Then he saw movement, over ad across the side parking lot, beside the dumpster. This person was walking towards him quite quickly, He shortly realized that it was Kenneth. "Kenneth. Are you ok?" Carl asked. "Can you take me to your house so I can explain everything to you?" Kenneth asked. "Yes and you can get a shower and I will give you some clothes. You can also have dinner with us." Carl stated. The ride home was quite silent. When they got home Kenneth went to the shower room, escorted by Carl. "Here are some clean clothes and towels." Carl said. Kenneth didn't say anything but just nodded. Carl went to the kitchen where Kerry was and said, "I think he was drinking. Why did he have blood in his hair?" Carl asked. "There are so many questions left un-answered right now honey, but, we cannot assume anything just yet.

We might let him stay just for tonight and then discuss everything in the morning." Kerry resounded. The room was silent now and Carl walked in and sat on the couch. Kerry was still in the kitchen. Kenneth walked out and went and sat next to Carl. Kenneth looked at Carl and said, "I really need your help. I know that I have hurt you and yes now I remorse for what I have done, but, right now I really need your help." Kenneth began crying. "It is really ok. remember we have forgiven you. You can stay the night here if you would like to." Carl told him. "I called you because your my friend. Now I know I can 100% trust and rely on you whenever I someone to talk to or need anything." Kenneth said through sobering sobs. "Well thank you Kenneth, but, I do have a question for you now. Why did you smell of alcohol, and why was there blood in your hair?" Carl asked. His head kind of tilted to the left a little. "Here is the story. For starters..." Kenneth began but Kerry interrupted by saying, "Dinner, come eat."

"We will finish this after dinner." Carl stated. After they ate dinner Kenneth and Carl went back to the family room. Kerry started cleaning up dinner, and doing the dishes. After Kerry was done there she joined in on the conversation. "Now we can finish discussing what happened to you or with you." Carl said, still confused, but, thanking God that he came to him. "Ok, well, here it goes. I hope that you believe me. I was in my room playing a video game, when dad came in. naturally drunk. He was always drunk. He has never ever gone thus far though. I think that he was dwelling on what happened. I don't know. I could be wrong. Anyways. I was sitting in my game chair with my headphone on, so it wouldn't be so loud for my mom to come upstairs and tell me to turn it down, when it all happened. It wasn't my mom. It was my dad. He burst in my room, I didn't hear him though. Grabs my chair and flips it over. He picks me up by my shirt and throws me into the wall. He then took his half empty beer bottle and broke it over my head while yelling at me because I didn't hear him knock." Kenneth stopped talking and started crying.

"It is ok now. Your safe here and nothing will happen to you in this house. I mean nothing." Carl said. Kerry didn't say anything. She just sat there with her hands over her mouth. "Do you want me to call the police? You do realize that is abuse and he will go to jail. I have seen the blood and can vouch for that. Do you have bruises or anything else anywhere?" Carl asked. "No, no, no. Please don't call the law. He will get even more angry with me when he gets out he might do something worse to me." Kenneth said in an elevated shaky tone that was a dead give away that he was scared out of his mind. "Has your dad ever hit you or laid a hand on you before tonight?" Carl asked. "NO sir." Kenneth retorted. Kind of offended that he would speak so awful about his dad, but then, he remembered he has to ask questions like that. "Kenneth. your a very bright young man and I know you know what you want, but, you have to gets worse?"

Well in this situation, your dad hit you. Now that he has hit you, he thinks that your not going to do anything about it for the simple fact of being scared. It will only get worse." Carl told Kenneth who was now n a full out bawl. "You can stay here tonight and in the morning we will take you back home if you don't want Carl to make that call. You have to really think about what you want to do though, because like Carl stated, it will only get worse unless you so something about it." Kerry said. "Ok, I will think about it. I do have one question for you. Why are you two so nice and so forgiving? I mean after what I did to you and your family? I mean I deserve to be put into jail and left there. Yet you had enough forgiveness to say what you said. The reason I never testified or gave my side of the story at the trial was because I knew that no matter what I said the judge was going to be making the final decision and I would have to deal with it. I also got off on a fair note also. Well, fair enough for what I did do." Kenneth then put his hands over his face with elbows perched on his knees.

Kerry and Carl both just looked at each other and smiled. "The reason we have so much forgiveness is because God has forgiven us and told us to forgive others. He told us to forgive seventy times seven. That equals out to be four hundred ninety times a day. Plus God has forgiven us in a way that only God could. God sent his one and only son, (Jesus) to die on the cross for our sins. Yes he did. So I found that if God has that much forgiveness then why can't we forgive others for their wrong doings? I mean, God forgave those who killed him, hurt him, called him names, hit him, spit on him, kicked him, beat him, whipped him, etc... So why can't man kind alike forgive someone that has even hit him?" Carl stated. "At first I had so much hatred towards the people that hurt my husband, but then, I had to stop and pray that God would soften my heart and renew my spirit and my mind set. Then I felt pity and compassion. Before you ask for forgiveness, you were already forgiven." Kerry said.

"Wow. I knew of God but despised him because I thought that he let bad things happen to get back at me for what I had done. I never knew all that." replied Kenneth. "I can tell you this. Once you learn of God and except him to be your personal Lord and Savior, it is not going to be an easy walk. I mean, there are several temptations in the world and trials that will come our way. God allows it to happen to strengthen your faith, trust and belief in him. You have to first love God and then love yourself, before you can even think or consider loving anyone else. So you are asking me, or Kerry, or both of us to help you, and lead you through the steps? We can't do it for you. After you except, God will take it from there, but, Kerry and I will be here to help guide and council you. If this is something you want. Your whole heart has to be in it or it is meaningless." Carl stated almost to the point of crying. Not in a bad but good way.

"Can I think about all of this and let you know in the morning what my decisions will be?" Kenneth asked. His eyes bounding between Kerry and Carl. "I think that that is a fantastic idea. You can sleep in the spare room. There is a bed in there." Carl stated. "Carl where are you going to sleep" Kerry whispered in Carl's ear. "With you my love." Carl stated back. There was noise in the kitchen at six-thirty a.m. Kerry got startled awake by it. "Carl. You need to go check and see what it might be." Kerry said. Carl, not ready to get up yet, rolled to the side of the bed and then put his pajama pants on and his robe and went to check. As Carl went downstairs to see what it was, he found Kenneth in the kitchen. "What are you doing?" Carl asked in a very tired voice. "I could hardly sleep last night. I kept thinking about what you said and I wanted to do something nice for you. I was going to make you both breakfast and coffee but I couldn't find anything. Sorry to have waken you up." Replied Kenneth.

Kerry was still in bed, waiting for Carl to come back and tell her what the noises were. forty-five minutes later, Carl comes back into the bedroom. "What was it dear?" Kerry asked. "It was Kenneth, trying to make breakfast and coffee for us." Carl stated. "Oh?" Kerry said questioningly. "Kenneth has the biggest gift of all for you. I guess more or less a huge surprise/gift." Carl said. Kerry got up and got dressed, as did Carl and then they walked downstairs. Kerry saw that the table was set and there was a note set on her plate. "Please Mrs. Benton, have a seat and I will serve you." Kenneth said excitedly. Kerry sat down and read the note.

Mrs. Benton,

You and Mr. Benton have been so generous to me. The good Lord revealed to me through you and Carl that I was going down the wrong path. I owe you so much because you and Carl and God have given me so much, and no longer will I ever take anything for granted again.

Sincerely,
Your brother in Christ,
Kenneth.

Kerry couldn't find any words to say. All she could do is stand to give her new found brother in Christ a big hug and all the while thanking God for it all and weeping.

Chapter 7

TIMES UP

That day Kerry, Carl and Kenneth all went down to the police station and turned his dad in. All Kerry and Carl wanted for Kenneth was for him to be safe. "So how long will he be in jail for?" Asked Kerry. The officer on this case now stated, "Well it al depends, if he wants to put in a no contact/restraining order or not. It also depends on how the living situations are." Kerry, the officer and Carl all looked at Kenneth for an answer. Carl piped up because he could sense that Kenneth was scared out of his mind for what he had just done. "He stays with us now." Kerry looked at Carl in disbelief that he just stated that. Kenneth looked at both of them and just started crying. The officer just gave all three of them a bewildered look. "Is that ok with your mom young man?" The officer wanted to know. "I will have to call her and tell her that I am safe and that I'm staying elsewhere now and to go get my clothes. Is there any way that a police officer can escort me there?" Kenneth asked with sobering sobs.

"I will have to do some checking around..." Before the officer could finish, Kerry interrupted her. "We will go out and get you some clothes. If your mom is that concerned we will have an officer, and not Carl, call her and tell her that you are safe and in a safe place. The officer will not state, by no means, where you are actually at. Would that be ok?" "Yes that would be wonderful." Stated Kenneth. The officer talking with them made the call and his mother seemed pleased to know. After they were done there, they went shopping for things that Kenneth needed. Upon returning home, Kerry helped Kenneth bring all the new stuff into his new room while he started putting it all away. "Thank you so much for everything." Kenneth said to Kerry as she brought in the last load. "Your more then welcome. You are more then welcome t stay as long as you would like also." Kerry walked out and back into the kitchen. Carl was already in the kitchen making dinner. "What are you making?" "Oh, tacos. Something easy, yet filling."

"You know the kids come home tomorrow." "Yeah. I know." "I wonder what they are going to say and think." Kerry stated. "No telling until we sit them both down in the living room and explain the situation. Would you feel more comfortable if Bill and Kim was here also?" "Yes, I would. You would allow that then?" "Yes dear. Why wouldn't I? They are family and family is always welcome in my home." Carl stated and looked at Kerry like she was kind of weird for asking that silly question. After dinner, Kerry asked if they would like to sit down and play a game or watch a movie. Them being men said movie. "What is it with men and not wanting to have fun with games? All you think is fun is mechanical stuff and things of that nature." "It is a mans sport. I mean mechanics. I know that women do it to, but, it just doesn't seem right." Carl said. They all sat down and watched the movie "The Passion Of The Christ." After the movie they all went to bed. Early the next morning, Carl heard a knock on the door. When he answered it, it was Bill and Kim bringing the kids home.

"Must have been a long night eh?" Bill said noticing that Carl had his pajama pants on and his bathrobe. "Yes. It was." Carl replied. "The kids are here, safe and sound." "I see that and little Jacob looks a lot darker then when he left. Did you have fun?" "Yes we did. Little Jacob bought souvenirs for everyone." "Ok cool. Hey listen. Kerry and i have some news for the kids and would like for you and Kim to be present as well." "Yeah ok. That would be fine." Bill replied. Carl went and got Kerry up and she came down, got hugs and kisses from the children and then sat them down, straight across from them. When they got almost done telling them what all took place when they were away, Kenneth came out of the room. Jacob didn't say anything but, slowly walked up to Kenneth and gave him a hug ad then stated, "Hello, brother. I always wanted a brother." "Well I could say the same." Kenneth said. Hailley didn't say anything, but instead went to her room. "Just give her time she will come around." Kerry said.

Months and months went by and church was going good and so was the community service. It was a week before a year was up. When court had its rule, it was that the boys had served their time and no more was to be added because upon entering the court, they all even saw all the changes in the boys. After they got done with court Kerry, Carl, Jacob, Hailley and Kennneth all went out to a pretty fancy restaurant to celebrate. "I'm so proud of you. All of you." Kerry said and Carl agreed.

Chapter 8

Seeing Through Different eyes

Later that night when Hailley and Jacob where in bed, Kerry and Carl sat Kenneth down on the couch. "We have never done this before but we would really like to help you get into college, beings that you only have two months before you graduate. Would you like us to or would you rather get a job temporary and help us?" Carl asked. "Mr. and Mrs. Benton. How about this. I don't know how you feel about it, but, I am going to throw this idea out there and see what you say about it." Kerry and Carl looked at each other and then at Kenneth, and said, "Ok, we are open to hear what you want to do. We are only here to help you grow and start heading in the right direction." "Thank you. I am truly grateful to hear that. You know, ever since I have asked God to be Lord of my life and to change me. I have had 100% complete trust and faith in Him that He would do so. This right here is truly proving it to me. I do truly want to go to college. Trust me I do. I see how you guys are and I have got a really good idea of how Carl does work and I would really like to see if I couldn't try and get into the precinct.

First I will have an I.O.U. on paper contract and then once I get my first job to start paying you back, little by little. I am not just going to take your money and run. Now if I was living like I was before, I probably would, but, now I wouldn't. God has eased my heart and is everyday showing and giving my spirit. Please allow me to help you out as much as you have helped me." Kenneth stated in a very sincere way. "If that is what you want to do then so be it. We will write out a contract for us all to do, and then, we will all sign it." So after all was said and done and the contract was inked and signed, they all shook hands and hugged in agreement to seal the written and verbal statement above. They all said good-night and Kenneth went into his room. Kerry and Carl just sat there and prayed.

Two months later, after going to Kenneth's graduation and to the party that they had for him at the house. Carl stood up and announced that, "We have some excellent news for you Kenneth. After talking with you that night, Kerry and I have been watching you very closely. We have seen your progress into a very strong young adult. So, I went to the precinct that I work for, and had a conversation with my boss, Sheriff Fang. He is willing to help pay for your classes but you have to get above a C in every class that you take or he will not even consider taking you into the precinct. I pulled some strings and asked if you could, after a year in college, go ahead and start working, in office, for the precinct, and he said yes." Every one clapped and hooted and hollard. Kenneth walked up to Carl and shook his hand and said, "Thank you very much sir." "I did my part. Now all you have to do is prove to the precinct and mostly to yourself, how bad you truly want this." Carl said.

Kenneth nodded in agreement. From the very first day at college, Kenneth took his studies seriously. When Kerry took the kids somewhere fun, Kenneth took all his school work. When he wanted a break he went and had some fun also. Three months after getting into class did Carl go up to Kerry and state, "He is doing one heck of a job. He is truly taking this all seriously. Do you see how he has changed, just in the amount of time of staying with us? I mean, even his outward appearance. He looks healthy and very clean cut." Carl said. "Yes dear. It is because he has two magnificent fathers who has taught him and is continuously still teaching him. I truly believe that he truly ad sincerely wants this." Kerry stated back. Already a year has passed since the first year of college, but, Kenneth still has one more year to go. Like Sheriff Fang promised, he allowed Kenneth to work in the office at the precinct for starters. His first day on the job did he come home and was talking to Carl about it. "Now you do remember that when you signed the confidentiality forms upon hire, you cannot tell anyone about anything. You can come to me as I work for the same precinct, but other than that nothing ok?" Carl said very seriously. Kenneth nodded and told him thank you very much for everything. "Imagine this. You only have one more year and you are a true police officer. How do you like it?" Carl asked. "It's good and I'm excited because now I understand why you told me that you fight for the safety of the community." Kenneth said. By this time Kerry was getting ready to have Jacobs seventh birthday party. Hailley was now in seventh grade. "Wow how the years fly by. What do we honestly do with the years and where do they go?" Kerry asked Carl. "Only God can answer that one. Right now we have to light the candles for Jacobs seven years that he has been alive." Carl said. After blowing the candles out, Jacob was asked if he wanted to do the cake and ice cream or his presents first.

He naturally said presents. When he was opening them Kerry took pictures of him holding up everything he got. From Hailley he got a signed baseball, glove, bat, ball, and extra balls so just in case he lost one. "Thanks Hailley." Jacob said and then hugged his sister. From Bill and Kim he got passes to the next big tournament in South Carolina, along with a plane ticket and all the fixings to go with it. Jacob who was so excited couldn't handle it. He jumped up, ran over and gave Bill and Kim a huge hug and said thanks. "I saw how much you really enjoyed the last one so I called and talked to your parents and they said ok, but not to make a habit of it." Bill said. When he opened the present from his mom and dad he saw that it was pretty small. He had always gotten big presents from them in the past but this one was different. It was a very expensive, Swivel, electric scooter. "Thanks mom and dad." He hugged them. He walked over to Kenneth and asked what he got him.

"Do you think that I would forget you, my little brother? Never." Kenneth said. He handed him a card. When Jacob opened it up he found seventy dollars in it and a card that read,

Dear Jacob,

I really hope that you are having a fantastic birthday. I also am having fun. Please except this as a token of thanks for being my younger brother and for excepting me for me.

Sincerely,
Kenneth.

P.S. Don't spend it all in one place. God bless and happy seventh birthday.

He hugged Kenneth and started crying. "Thanks bro. Your awesome. Trust me I won't spend it all in one place." They both giggled. Upon working for the precinct another year, Kenneth had his first day in the field. His first day consisted of working with D.U.I. people, giving tickets, giving drug tickets, car searches and one fatality. When he got home from work, he sat Carl down and said. "I now realize how much you truly do. I can almost see through your eyes, but in a different way. Thank you so much." "Your welcome. Just remember one thing. When scared to death ask God to help you and give you the strength and he will. After praying don't show fear to anyone. Offenders usually go after the weak." "Wow. Ok thanks for the tips." Kenneth said. A few months has passed now and work was going good for everyone when Kerry started not to feel very good. She had to take a lot of time off work, so that meant that the boys had to work extra hard. Carl came home and told Kerry that Kenneth was shot in the line of duty.

He was taken to the hospital. Kerry went with Carl and was also checked out. Carl went in to see Kenneth. The first words out of his mouth was, "I'm so sorry for what I had done to you and your family. Thank you for forgiving me." A few moments later the cardiac machine went to a straight line. Kenneth died right there in Carl's arms on April 15, 2002 and 2:22 p.m. Carl didn't know what to say or anything. So he went to Kerry's room and talked with her. "He's dead Kerry." Carl said in a shocked manor. "Don't fret Carl, he is with God now." Kerry said smiling. "Why are you smiling Kerry?" Asked Carl. "I know that he is with God and we are going to have another baby."

ABOUT THE AUTHOR

I was born and raised in Tenino Washington. I lived with my parents until I was 17. Tenino is a small town, so everyone knew pretty much about everyone else. I played a lot of sports to keep me out of trouble, not only that, but it kept me in shape. My favorite sport was a toss up from fast pitch and volleyball. Track and cross-country was ok, but if you know what those sports are, then you know that you get winded pretty easily, beings that they are running sports. Basketball was ok but not my forte. When I wasn't playing then I was playing in the band for the games. When I was 20, I was in a really bad car wreck that could have taken my life. Thank God it didn't though because I would have missed out on the gifts that God gave me.

Found out that I was pregnant at age 21 and had him on September 30th 2004. He was a blessing. I was always told that when I was younger that I Would make a great mom.

When I did tell my parents that I was pregnant they changed their minds and told me that I needed help. I then proceeded to tell them that it was a boy and they told me that it was going to make it doubly hard. At this point in my life I was scared. I have to admit that one, but then again who isn't with their first child. I was told my by parents that I needed to give the baby up because I was single and at that time wouldn't be a good mother. I didn't listen to them. When the time came for delivery, my mom told me that she is glad that I didn't listen to her because he was handsome, and then told me that he looked like his dad. That made me mad. That is not something that I wanted to hear considering the fact of I wasn't with the dad.

When Christian was 3, I got married and pregnant with another son. I knew that the name had to be Ezzekiel. I wanted all Christian names for my children to present themselves as to who I admired from the Bible. Ezzekiel was born on July 18th 2007, 5 weeks early and almost didn't make it. His left lung collapsed and had to have surgery to get it back up and going again. I couldn't touch him for 6 weeks and I couldn't hold him for another 2 weeks. That was the hardest days of my life. I was in constant prayer. I was also going through a rough time with my husband. 4 weeks after I had Ezzekiel I found out that I was pregnant with my daughter. She was born on June 27, 2008. She was supposed to be born on July 18 but didn't make it that long but earlier. Her name is Hadassah. She was named after queen Esther out of the Bible.

The year of 2011, was the next hardest year of my life. I got divorced from my husband and then 4 weeks later got my children taken away from me, after asking for just help. I lost my mind so I got into my car and drove. I ended up in Tennessee where I had friends that I stayed with. Then I moved to Florida and met my hopefully soon to be husband in August of 2012. We have been together since. He is a good, hard working, good provider, tries to make sure that all is taken care of financially. His name is Timothy. What inspired me to write is an author by the name of James Patterson. He is almost the only author that I read. I would have to say that my favorite book from him is You've Been Warned. Very inspiring. I would like to get all of the books that he has wrote.

To sum up about me, I would have live by the old saying that things only get better. That is how I lived my life. I went from a bad living situation to a good one, then back to a horrible one and now getting back on track to a fantastic one. I do miss my children dearly, but I know one day that I will have them back and never let go of them again. If it wasn't for them and God, I honestly don't think that I would still be alive today.

Special Thanks

I want to first of all, thank God for giving me the words to write and visions to actually see my book as it was being wrote. I'm not an author by no means, but with the help and the words of Christ it is all possible. You just have to open your heart, your mind, ears and listen and watch what the good Lord has to show you. So he would be my first thanks. My friends kept telling me that I could do it. That was awesome because when I was down, I didn't know if I really could but thanks to them and their kind words, I finally did it. Thank you God for giving the words and visions. Thank you Christian C., Ezzekiel H., Hadassah H., Timothy B., and James Patterson. You have all been very good to me and gave me the words that I needed to hear and the words that needed to be wrote. Thank you from the bottom of my heart. Thank God that God didn't allow me to not write this book because if so then I would be fearful of getting mocked, ridiculed and much worse, put to death for my faith. The good Lord gave me the courage I needed to stand tall and have no fear of telling people what the name of my book is and that it was a Christian book.

I would have to say that if you haven't read it make sure and read it. My favorite book in the Bible is Ecc. 3. It is very true, everything does have a time under the heavens and only in God's time will it happen. God is so good and that is why I thank him. Without him this book would not be out today. Thank you God. God bless and may God be with you the rest of your days and if not then contact me and I will help with that situation. Thank you God. Amen.